HOW TO WIN OVER WORRY

JOHN EDMUND HAGGAI

HARVEST HOUSE PUBLISHERS

EUGENE, OREGON

Unless otherwise indicated, all Scriptures are taken from the King James Version of the Bible.

Verses marked Phillips are taken from J.B. Phillips: The New Testament in Modern English, Revised Edition. © J.B. Phillips 1958, 1960, 1972. Used by permission of Macmillan Publishing Company.

Verses marked AMP are taken from The Amplified Bible, Old Testament, Copyright © 1965 and 1987 by The Zondervan Corporation, and from The Amplified New Testament, Copyright © 1954, 1958, 1987 by The Lockman Foundation. Used by permission.

Cover by Harvest House Publishers, Corey Fisher, designer

HOW TO WIN OVER WORRY
Copyright © 2001 by John Edmund Haggai
Published by Harvest House Publishers
Eugene, Oregon 97402

Library of Congress Cataloging-in-Publication Data

Haggai, John Edmund.
    How to win over worry / John Edmund Haggai.—Updated.
        p. cm.
    ISBN-13: 978-0-7369-1753-7
    ISBN-10: 0-7369-1753-5
    1. Worry—Religious aspects—Christianity. 2. Christian life. I. Title.
BV4908.5.H3 2001
248.4—dc21   00-053913

Printed in the United States of America

06 07 08 09 10 11 12 13 / BP-MS / 10 9 8 7 6 5 4 3 2 1

*Dedicated to Carl and Janie Newton
of San Antonio, Texas,
personal envoys of Christ Jesus
and cherished friends.*

CONTENTS

Part 4: PRAYER

Part 5: PEACE

PREFACE

More than 50 years ago, I began to deliver an address entitled "How to Win Over Worry." No matter where I delivered this address, the attendance exceeded all other attendances. It became clear that I had touched upon a felt need. Thousands of people who attended these services requested a copy of the address.

In 1958, my wife and my associate collaborated in putting pressure on me to reduce the address to print. They suggested I make this the lead address in a book of a dozen major sermons and addresses.

In late 1958, I set aside three weeks to accomplish this purpose. The more I wrote on the subject of worry, the more it seemed to expand. At the end of three weeks, I had finished a 200-page book devoted exclusively to the subject. And in May of 1959, the first copies of *How to Win Over Worry* appeared in bookstores across America.

It was the first of this genre published by a Christian publishing house and released in Christian bookstores. The publisher showed great courage in promoting this book. He intended, as I later found out, to let it run for a year or so, then put it on sale, and discontinue its production.

How this book became a bestseller

Two developments kept the book alive. One of the publisher's sales representatives announced to Oregon bookstore owner Bob Hawkins, Sr. the publisher's intention to discontinue the book after the present edition was exhausted. Bob Hawkins owned two bookstores in the state at the time. He said, "That book cannot go out of print." In vigorous terms, he gave reasons why it must be reprinted. To prove his point of the book's importance, he ordered

500 hardback copies. For the average bookstore dealer at the time, purchasing 500 hardback copies for two modest-sized bookstores in a modest-sized city would be foolhardy. Bob sold all of the books within two months.

In the meantime, I had spoken to Mr. Ellison, who had paperback book concessions in 92 of America's leading airports. Ellison requested the book be put in paperback so that he could sell it in the airports. The book sold well.

What Bob Hawkins did for this book and Ellison did for its paperback edition launched its permanence. Had I known of the publisher's plan in 1959 not to reprint my book, I'm sure I never would have written another book. Since Bob's purchase of those 500 copies of the book, it has been translated into 19 languages, gone through more than 50 printings, and sold over 2,000,000 copies. It has touched the lives of readers in more than 150 countries.

I am pleased that Harvest House, founded by Bob Hawkins, Sr., and now headed by his son Bob Hawkins, Jr., is publishing this new edition for the new millennium.

A remarkable story about Win Over Worry

As these lines are being printed, I have reached my ninth decade of life. For more than 60 of my 80-plus years, I have been before the public on every continent and in scores of nations. I have completed nearly 100 trips around the world, in addition to nearly 200 intercontinental trips. All of that to say that over more than half a century of time, I have found that human nature does not change. In upgrading the statistics for chapter 1, I have been amazed that in America the need to help people cope with the problem of worry has increased alarmingly.

South African Andre Petersie, who became a top executive with one of Hollywood's leading film companies, phoned me one day to request that I send the book on worry to a friend of his in London, a leading impresario in the United Kingdom. In less than a week after I had sent the book, I received a phone call from London. The name was strange to me until I realized that this was the man that Petersie asked me to help.

The impresario said, "I want to thank you for the book. I was in the bedroom of my London residence, gun in hand, ready to blow out my brains when I heard a thud downstairs. It got my attention. I looked over the balcony railing to see that a parcel had been put through the mail slot. Curiosity drove me to find out what was in the parcel before I ended my life. It was your book. As a result, there has been a transformation of my life. I have turned it over completely to the Lord Jesus Christ, and I want to thank you for being the instrument to save me not only physically, but also spiritually."

What can reading this book achieve?

This book makes no claim to deal with psychiatric and medical problems. What it does is present a formula for assisting people who are afflicted with anxiety, but who do not suffer from the kind of mental illness that requires professional medical intervention.

After the fifth edition of this book was released, I addressed the Texas Medical Association and found that more than 100 of the doctors were using the book for mildly disturbed patients. Hundreds of clergymen and counselors, both in the United States and overseas, have used the book to help those coming to them for assistance.

I believe that worry is an underlying condition of American society—and probably global society also. Not everyone suffers from clinical depression or psychosis. But everyone, at some time, will worry. And many will find that uncontrolled worry corrodes the joy of living and brings about a deterioration of mind and body.

Of course it is naïve to expect that reading one book one time will ever, by itself, produce a total life-change. An outstanding Memphis soprano soloist who read *How to Win Over Worry* told me, "I have read your book, and I am still worrying."

I said, "Ruth, I know you are not too touchy about your age, so tell me how old you are."

Perplexed, she said, "Fifty-three. Why?"

"Am I to conclude that you have been worrying for most of your 53 years?"

"Yes, I have."

"Don't you think it's a bit illogical to think that with one reading of a book that just may have the answer to your problem, you can override 53 years of habit?"

I do not hold out any hope for anybody who reads the book just once. I myself reread it periodically to reinforce the truths that I need for my own emotional health and vitality—and I am the author!

I suggest you read it and reread it. Make notes in the margins or inside the back cover about passages that have special relevance to your need. And write out specific goals. The New York psychiatrist Ari Kiev discovered that patients who set goals and worked toward their fulfillment did much better than those who did not. Goals that are specific and time-sensitive, and broken down into action steps, will give you a real sense of control over your problem and help you climb out of it.

Finally, you will see very soon that the advice this book offers is distilled from another far greater book—the Bible. When I was a young man, I heard a clinical psychologist say, "What you think about the first five minutes after you awaken will determine the kind of day you have." I cannot recommend strongly enough that anyone surrounded by worry make time every morning to read the only truly life-changing book that has ever been written.

Part 1
PROBLEM

1
WHY WORRY?

At age 24 I suffered a nervous breakdown.

At the time I was serving full-time as minister of a church. Simultaneously I was taking 19 college hours and conducting evangelistic campaigns. Conscientious, determined, and energetic, I drove myself into the ground.

Everyone felt sorry for me—my wife, my congregation, my doctor. But believe me, no one felt as sorry as I felt for myself. I was miserable. Finally the doctor ordered me to get away for several weeks of rest and diversion—a break that my church graciously made possible.

During those weeks of convalescence I arrived at a liberating conclusion. I came to understand that my condition did not arise from any mental or physical disorder. Nor was it the result of my heavy workload. The problem lay in my attitude. I'd been doing something wrong. I'd been *worrying*.

With gratitude to God, I can say that since the fall of 1948 I have not lost five minutes' sleep over any problem, difficulty, tension, or adverse circumstance. I've faced the same challenges in life as any other person. Probably more. But nothing makes me anxious. In a matter of a few days I learned to win over worry. That lesson has lasted me a lifetime.

Worry is the #1 disorder

Worry is eating the vitality of America. Anxiety disorders—more serious mental problems that spring out of worry—are the nation's most common psychiatric condition. About 25 million Americans experience anxiety disorders. The risk of developing an anxiety disorder is about 25 percent—and double that if you're a woman.

According to the National Mental Health Association, anxiety disorders cost the United States an astonishing $46.6 billion each year—nearly *one-third* of the nation's total mental health bill. Thanks to worry and related mental problems, the U.S. economy loses an estimated $79 billion every year in lost productivity. Globally, according to the World Health Organization, mental disorders in the developed world account for more than 15 percent of the economic burden of disease.

Not every mental disorder has a simple solution. On the other hand, it's striking how often serious mental illness has its roots in everyday stress situations. It's also striking how much worry and unhappiness these same situations cause to people who do not think of themselves as mentally ill.

Life throws worries at us from every direction:

1. *Growing up is worrying.* Growing up is hard enough by itself—with worries ranging from imagined bears in the bedroom to terrifying bullies at school. Increases in divorce and single parenting have only increased the stress. A 1996 study by MECA (Methodology for Epidemiology of Mental Disorders in Children and Adolescents) estimated that almost 21 percent of U.S. children ages 9 to 17 had a clear mental or addictive disorder. The Center for Mental Health Services reports that "at any given time, as many as one in

every 33 children may have clinical depression. The rate of depression among adolescents may be as high as one in eight."

2. *Work is worrying.* Worries at work plague many people. Most people have worries at work. Some professions have achieved notoriety for producing stress. Air-traffic controllers have more stomach ulcers than any other professionals. Company directors suffer the highest incidence of death from heart disease, duodenal ulcers, suicide, and strokes. Other high-stress occupations include commodity brokers, emergency services, local government, social services, all kinds of shift work, sales and marketing, teaching, tele-sales, and medical care. As one leading medical doctor put it, "Business people who don't know how to fight worry die young."

3. *Being a woman is worrying.* A recent national survey of 1,044 American women showed that 56 percent reported experiencing anxiety symptoms and worry for a period of more than six months. More than one in four of the women reported muscle aches and pains, muscle tension, irritability, and being easily fatigued. One in five said they have trouble sleeping at night because they "worry about things." Twenty-nine percent reported that worry and anxiety symptoms caused trouble in their relationships with their spouse, friends, parents, or co-workers.

4. *Having a home and family is worrying.* All kinds of domestic responsibilities bring stress. Parents routinely worry about children experimenting with drugs or getting into bad company. And domestic

worry seems to be getting worse. In 1999, 6 in 10 Americans said they worried more about the safety of children than they had a year before. Within this group, 37 percent (74 million adults) said they worried "a lot more." One in eight Americans (about 26 million people) felt more fearful of walking in their neighborhoods than they had a year earlier.

5. *Past experiences are worrying.* People commonly look back on some past event and worry about it. Something they could have said better. Something they wish they hadn't done. In addition, America seems to be seeing a surge in post-traumatic stress disorder (PTSD). Nineteen years after combat exposure, 15 percent of Vietnam veterans were found to be suffering from PTSD—a figure that may rise as they get older.

6. *Getting older is worrying.* Older people easily turn into worriers. They feel less in control, and more uncertain about the future. Studies show that in any one year over 11 percent of those age 55 and over will suffer some form of anxiety disorder, including phobias and feelings of panic. More general feelings of worry are reported in up to 17 percent of older men and 21 percent of older women.

Like smoking, worry attacks your health

A friend in the ministry, Eddie Lieberman, once had to help a young woman who'd become paralyzed. He went to see her. She told him she was sick, that she didn't love her husband anymore (he was overseas in the Armed Forces at the time), and that she wanted a divorce. Her physical state was deteriorating badly.

Eddie Lieberman had trained in psychology, and his instincts as a psychologist told him something was drastically wrong with this girl. He requested permission to admit her to Duke University Hospital. There the true story came out.

Her problems had begun with a letter from her husband. He said he'd fallen in love with another girl. It was he, not she, who wanted to initiate divorce proceedings. Her severe, untreated anxiety had produced the physical symptoms of paralysis.

Eddie Lieberman tried to help her, but she was so deeply mired in the breakdown of her marriage that she had no will to be helped. She should have been a lively, vivacious woman in her mid-thirties. Instead she was a morose paralytic bound for a premature grave. The culprit: worry.

Research has long shown the link between worry and ill health. The April 1998 *Harvard Mental Health Letter* says that "research on the relationship between health and emotion indicates that stress affects the body at the cellular level in ways that increase risk of disease. Stress is linked to heart disease and hypertension and may play a role in cancer."

Susan Barr and Jerilynn Prior of the University of British Columbia in Vancouver, Canada, recently questioned 51 healthy pre-teen girls about weight worries. They also measured the mineral content of the girls' bones using low-dose X-rays. They were surprised to find that worry about weight linked directly to bone density. The more worried the girl, the more likely it was that her bone density would be low—putting her at a significantly higher risk of osteoporosis.

Where to find the answer to worry

Modern psychiatry has studied anxiety for over 100 years. But it has not, on the whole, found any reliable treatment for it. When I needed answers to anxiety, therefore, I did not look to the medical profession. I went to the New Testament. In the Bible you find a completely different analysis of worry—and a completely different solution to it.

New Testament Greek scholars correctly translate the Greek verb "to worry" with the words, "to take thought," "to be anxious," and "to be careful." That Greek verb—*merimnao*—fuses two other words—*merizo*, meaning "to divide," and *nous*, meaning "mind" (a term which includes the faculties of perceiving, understanding, feeling, judging, and determining).

In the thinking of the New Testament, then, worry implies "a divided mind." There is no unity of thought or action. Part of you tugs in one direction; another part of you strains to move in another direction. You are like a trailer with a car pulling from each end. No wonder the apostle James concludes, "A double-minded man is unstable in all his ways" (James 1:8).

When you worry, you express a conflict of purpose. Consequently you become unstable. James goes further. He says you become unstable *in all your ways*. Every part of your mind—that part of you that is supposed to coordinate your being and keep you "together"—is in danger of becoming unstable. You become unstable in your emotions. Unstable in your thought processes. Unstable in your decisions. Unstable in your judgments.

- Worry divides your FEELINGS— causing your emotions to become uneven and volatile.

- Worry divides your UNDERSTANDING—making your convictions lose their grounding, sapping you of confidence.

- Worry divides your PERCEPTION—meaning you are distracted and often fail to see the whole situation confronting you.

- Worry divides your JUDGMENT—making your decisions ill-informed and unreliable.

- Worry divides your WILL—producing lethargy and dulling your ability to pursue your goals with determination.

Worry causes heartbreak, failure, misunderstanding, suspicion, and much unhappiness. And left long enough, this division of the mind can be so severe that you can no longer muster the energy to struggle against your problems. Then your mind will do something computers sometimes do—crash. The system gets overloaded. There's no room left to sort anything out. So it freezes. It shuts down. You go through a nervous breakdown or develop symptoms of a severer mental disorder.

The divided mind is the source of the problem

Look at the kinds of personal problems that cause people to worry. It's not long before you can see the divided mind behind it.

For example, marital breakdown directly expresses the loss of "single-minded" devotion to a relationship. The husband's affections may become divided between his wife and another woman. It may be that the wife's loyalty is divided between her husband and her mother. A parent's will and attention can be divided between responsibilities to children and responsibilities to the spouse. A wage earner may divide his—or her—mind between the needs of family and the driving ambition to succeed in a career.

The divided mind can afflict children. Who can determine the percentage of school failures caused by a divided mind? I grew up in a preacher's home, and I know how intense the pressures can be. If you are a "model child," you get held up by other parents as a pattern for their own kids to emulate—with the result that your friends detest you. On the other hand, if you give in to your natural bent for mischief, you win the respect of your friends—but the wrath of your parents.

I have a brother who was so sensitive about being a preacher's son that he deliberately made poor grades so his friends wouldn't think of him as a "goody-goody." He had an excellent mind—a fact later proved by his collegiate scholastic records. In the end he graduated with honors in electrical engineering at one of the nation's leading universities. In 1971, he was given the L. A. Hyland award for scientific achievement. He led the group that produced and launched Syncom Satellite. Much of the work done to produce the detection and communications components of the AWACS planes took place in his department under his leadership. But during high school, he let worry ruin his performance.

In many cases the outcomes reveal far greater damage. Barely a day goes by when we don't hear about children failing at school because their minds are on discord at home. Neglect distracts them. Sometimes they are actually forced to choose between parents. Consequently they soon feel unwanted, and express this by creating havoc at school. They are seeking the attention and affection their family denies them.

Or look at the business world. Only the Lord knows how many businesses have been torpedoed by the divided mind. In the late 1920s, an uneducated European immigrant opened a hot-dog stand. His business grew. He expanded. Soon he owned a chain of stands. His income soared at a time when unemployment hit 25 percent. He sent his son to the university where he graduated with a major in Business Administration. The father proudly brought him into the business.

The son said, "You know, Dad, there's a depression on. Business is bad everywhere. Many businesses have gone into bankruptcy. We must be careful. Let's cut down our inventory, reduce our advertising budget, lay off some of the help, and tighten our belts."

Against his better judgment, the father listened to his "learned" son and followed the advice. Yes, you've guessed it. The son succeeded in dividing his father's mind between the principles of success that had made him wealthy during the Great Depression and the possibility of bankruptcy. Soon their business folded. Worse yet, depressed by the financial reverses, the father lost his sparkle, his "drive," his optimistic outlook, and began to deteriorate physically.

One of the most bitter and cynical men I have ever known was a man loaded with talent. He had more ability than any six of his peers. He could have been a leading cartoonist, a top-notch photographer, a highly paid after-dinner speaker, a humorist, a prosperous realtor, a topflight hotel executive, or a celebrated writer. But he failed to achieve any worthwhile accomplishment or even earn a decent living. He became an embarrassment to family and friends.

He saw men without a fraction of his ability soar to the heights of success while he groveled in the "Slough of Despond." Those who knew him and loved him knew the reason: a divided mind. He never came to the point of determining what he was going to do. He could not say with Paul the apostle, "This one thing I do." He would never throw all of his energies into a single project. He aimed at nothing, hit a bull's-eye, and then brooded over the result.

What a waste. He became critical of others who did achieve. He would rationalize his failure and deal out misery to his associates. Worry, born of indecision, stripped him of his influence, and soon his health.

So what are you going to do about it?

The refrain of a famous blues number tells us:

> *It takes a worried man to sing a worried song.*
> *I'm worried now—but I won't be worried long.*

Well, that's a pious hope. Worry is endemic. It infiltrates businesses and brings them crashing down. It roars through homes like a tornado, leaving in its wake smashed family relationships—bitter and frustrated parents, and insecure, emotionally damaged children. It drives some to spend fortunes on psychotherapy and others into psychiatric care. In America, at least, worry has virtually become part of the national culture. You could write on countless gravestones in nations all over the world this epitaph:

> *Hurried*
> *Worried*
> *Buried*

Everyone would like to say, "I'm worried now, but I won't be worried long." But what's going to change? One definition of insanity is, "Expecting a different result while doing the same thing."

Problems don't go away. It's naïve to think that the world around you will suddenly resolve into serene bliss. It's equally naïve to think that a new job or a new relationship will lift you safely above your troubles. They won't. If you're worried now, I can guarantee you that you'll be worried in five or ten years' time—even if you've won the lottery or married a world-class celebrity. At best all you'll do is swap one set of problems for another.

I know from my own experience that there is one, and only one, sure solution to worry. God delineates the solution in the Bible. I'll start to unpack it in chapter 3. First of all, though, let's see why other remedies for worry simply don't work.

2
A TOTAL SOLUTION

A friend recently noticed ants in his kitchen.

At first it was just one or two, and he ignored them, assuming they'd crept in from the garden through an open window. But then they got more numerous. Spurred to action by the complaints of his family (the ants had found the cookie jar), he began going around and squashing them with his thumb. This worked for about three hours. It soon became clear, however, that the ants were reproducing themselves more quickly than he could squash them. Further, by the following day they were clearly organized, and were marching in lines toward any available food source.

My friend was forced to move vulnerable food into the refrigerator. Soon the refrigerator was stuffed to capacity, and he had to resort to balancing the leftovers in the middle of dishes of water, rather like a castle with a moat around it. In no time these fortifications occupied every counter. But to no avail. Still the ants came. The kitchen simply had too many specks of food around it. It could not be kept clean. For one thing, the children could not be relied on to sweep up every crumb after themselves, and my friend did not have time to follow them around with a dustpan and a can of disinfectant.

Within a week the ants seemed to have taken over the kitchen. They were coming out from every crack in the baseboards—too many places to stop up with wet plaster or tape. They hid their nests deep in the wall cavity. My friend could not reach them without first removing all the kitchen units and digging up the floor. He had only one option left—the only option guaranteed to work. He covered the area with a powerful ant poison. By the next weekend, every ant was gone.

Flattery will get you nowhere

As my friend discovered, problems need a total solution. The easiest thing—the least troublesome or costly measure—may be next to useless. And so it is with worry. All kinds of knee-jerk reactions recommend themselves when we're feeling anxious. Sure, you may kill a few ants. Sure, you may keep a few shelves ant-free. But long-term, nothing's really changed. To win, you've got to deal with the problem at its source. Everything else is a waste of your time.

Take flattery. You flatter others if you want to keep them from hurting you. So people with fragile egos, and people who are afraid of others criticizing them, use flattery as a means of self-protection. It functions like a bribe. You tell the other person what you think he or she wants to hear in the hopes that this will neutralize the hostility he or she may harbor towards you.

Of course, if you do that, you are playing mind games. At best, flattery is a short-term fix. If the other person really is hostile, flattery won't keep the hostility at bay for very long. And if there is no hostility, then you are sowing the seeds of your own undoing. For how can you secure the lasting good opinion of others by telling them lies? Insincerity shows. Consequently, someone who might otherwise have thought well of you will be driven into suspicion and resentment. Worry reaps its own reward.

Not surprisingly, the Word of God denounces flattery over 30 times.

Job says, "He that speaketh flattery to his friends, even the eyes of his children shall fail" (Job 17:5). And, "Let me not, I pray you, accept any man's person; neither let me give flattering titles unto man. For I know not to give flattering titles; in so doing my Maker would soon take me away" (Job 32:21,22).

The psalmist records the sinfulness and foolishness of flattery in Psalm 5:9: "For there is no faithfulness in their mouth . . . they flatter with their tongue." Also: "They speak vanity every one with his neighbor: with flattering lips and with a *double heart* do they speak" (Psalm 12:2).

The wisest man of history, Solomon, admonishes us: "He that goeth about as a talebearer revealeth secrets: therefore meddle not with him that flattereth with his lips" (Proverbs 20:19). "A lying tongue hateth those that are afflicted by it; and a flattering mouth worketh ruin" (Proverbs 26:28).

It doesn't take much size to criticize

This old saying is true. Criticism, as a solution to worry, leads the worrier up another blind alley. Criticizing others seems to help us, for three reasons:

- First, when we criticize we feel good. We get to feel we're standing on the moral high ground—a position where everyone else will look up to us.

- Second, when we criticize we project our misery onto others. If everyone else is miserable too, we feel less conspicuous. It also takes our mind off our own problems, at least for a short time.

- Third, when we criticize we create the illusion that we have overcome the thing that worries us—by condemning the same thing in someone else.

Of course, criticizing is childish. It brings only temporary relief. And—tragically—it further focuses our minds upon negative thoughts, and the mischief that inevitably follows negative thinking only adds to our worries and intensifies the depression.

It is true that "what Peter says about Paul tells more about Peter than it does about Paul." Or, in the words of the little couplet:

> *Things that thou dost in others see*
> *Are the most prevalent in thee.*

The Bible tells us that to the impure, all things are impure (Titus 1:15). Similarly, to the dishonest, all things are dishonest. To the untrue, all things are untrue. When the worrier criticizes others, he solves none of his own worries. Instead he focuses his attention upon the miserable traits he sees in others, which mirror his own condition. Thus riveted to a destructive and negative pattern of thought, he further supplements his already overstocked supply of fears.

Paul the apostle denounces the sin of criticism when in Romans 2:1 he says, "Therefore thou art inexcusable, O man, whatsoever thou art that judgest: for wherein thou judgest another, thou condemnest thyself; for thou that judgest doest the same things." What the worrier fails to realize is that in criticizing others he reveals to the world the very problem he is trying to conceal.

Frenetic activity fails to establish a refuge from worry

Another useless response to worry is to throw yourself into *excessive activity*. Work occupies the attention; it keeps the mind from straying onto painful thoughts. But it has no power to take pain away. When you finish your shift, or come home from the office, your problems still hound you. Unhappily, you now have less, not more, energy to deal with them.

Frenetic activity allows only a temporary escape. You postpone your appointment with anxiety. But you cannot put it off forever. Nor can you produce worthwhile results with your worries simmering underneath the surface. People who work to hide worry often give the appearance of being busy. Truth is, they don't accomplish much of substance. They are like worms on a hot rock, or as one TV personality put it, they are as "nervous as a long-tailed cat in a room full of rocking chairs."

An astounding number of people in senior positions work themselves into the ground in an effort to suppress worry. They embody the modern-day beatitude, "Blessed are they that go around in circles, for they shall be called big wheels." Feverish activity, motivated by the desire to escape rather than the urge to produce, solves nothing. It can briefly take the mind off the fear-producing thoughts that cause anxiety. But in the long run it is counterproductive. It actually multiplies problems, and thereby intensifies the very condition it was expected to solve.

There is a place of refuge from worry, as Jesus suggested to His disciples: "Come ye yourselves apart into a desert place, and rest a while" (Mark 6:31). But that refuge does not lie in frenetic activity. People who busy themselves to forget their worries enjoy no sense of peace. Most of them could not stand their own company for 30 minutes without the aid of a diversion like television, radio, books, or a video. They take sleeping pills to get a night's rest, and pep pills to get started in the morning. To make it through the day, they stay tanked up on caffeine.

Self-righteous resignation embraces no virtue

Another ineffective strategy against worry is to give in to it—and to present this as a sort of heroism.

Of course it is nothing of the kind. There is nothing heroic about buckling under to something you see as inevitable. Yet it's common to hear people speak as though worries were medals won in the heat of battle—and ulcers are the badge of their conscientiousness.

They will assert, "My cross is heavy, but I am determined to bear it valiantly."

This is almost blasphemous. Wherever the biblical injunction "Take up thy cross" appears, it refers to death to sin and death to self. This is the exact antithesis of putting up with worry. The Bible never refers to any problem, grief, or dilemma as a cross, nor does it commend people with worries as though they were called to some special service. The person who *really* bears a cross knows no worry. He has died to sin and to self. Thus he insulates himself from destructive fears. He has peace because his mind is firmly set upon Christ.

Jesus never complained about the weight of His cross. And yet His cross, the real instrument of death, and not just a metaphor, imposed a physical suffering none of us could endure with grace.

Following His example, our Lord's disciples rejoiced that "they were counted worthy to suffer shame for His name" (Acts 5:41). By contrast, people who respond to worry, fear, and anxiety with a self-righteous resignation say one thing, but live another. They delude no one but themselves. Although they claim to bring glory to God, their faces would "draw a wart on a tombstone."

Their biblical model isn't Jesus at all. It is Jonah, sulking outside Nineveh and saying, "Therefore now, O LORD, take, I beseech thee, my life from me; for it is better for me to die than to live" (Jonah 4:3). Or Elijah, fleeing from Jezebel: "It is enough; now, O LORD, take away my life; for I am not better than my fathers" (1 Kings 19:4c). (I always chuckle when I read this passage. If Elijah had stayed in Jezebel's city, she would long since have granted his petition!)

Don't mistake this for spiritual heroism. Call it by its name: cowardice, and unbecoming self-pity. Instead of tackling the problem head on— correcting the thought patterns, and taking corrective action—the worrier sits down and moans.

Dope won't help you cope

Alcohol, cigarettes, and narcotics all lead the worrier into the same dead end.

Who can calculate the damage done by the many plays, TV dramas, and movies that portray the unrequited lover desperately hitting the corner bar to drink away his sorrows? When trouble comes, too many people seek comfort in some form of drug.

The idea that a drunken spree opens up an escape hatch from an agonizing situation produces pernicious results. The Japanese say, "A man takes a drink, then the drink takes a drink, and the drink takes the man."

Solomon, the sage of the ages, speaks wisely when he says, "Who hath woe? Who hath sorrow? Who hath contentions? Who hath babbling? Who hath wounds without cause? Who hath redness of eyes? They that tarry long at the wine; they that go to seek mixed wine" (Proverbs 23:29,30).

It is still true that "wine is a mocker, strong drink is raging: and whosoever is deceived thereby is not wise" (Proverbs 20:1). Three millennia later, the only thing that's changed is the variety of chemicals at our disposal. Alcohol now comes in hundreds of different packages. So does nicotine. If these fail, we can obtain any number of more powerful narcotics—legal or otherwise.

They all have the same effect. Temporary exhilaration diverts the mind from fear-producing thoughts. Then the sufferer is unceremoniously dumped back where he or she was at the beginning—except, in many cases, with a headache. This pattern of behavior only postpones the problem and ultimately increases the pain.

Positive thinking gets you only halfway there

Some worriers resort to yet another solution—seeking to conquer worry by positive thinking.

Now, positive thinking is good. Certainly a person cannot have positive thoughts and fear-producing thoughts at the same time. The question is whether the program of positive thinking supplies us with the "fuel" we need to move forward. It is one thing to know what we ought to do. It is another thing to have the ability to do it.

In a way it is the same dilemma produced by the Ten Commandments. They showed humanity what to be and what to do. But nobody—the Lord Jesus Christ excepted—has ever actually succeeded in keeping them. There's a world of difference between reading the rulebook and living by the rules.

With all of my heart, I believe in the power of positive thinking. Let it be understood, however, that God alone is the source of positive thoughts. Paul says in 2 Timothy 1:7, "For God hath not given us the spirit of fear; but of power, and of love, and of a sound mind."

Positive thinking is a counterfeit solution if it lures us into thinking that we—in our own strength and by our own resources—can bring about the shift in mental attitude necessary to banish fear and worry. You might just as well try to shoot an African lion with a water pistol as try to conquer worry with a self-inspired and self-produced positive attitude.

Positive thinking needs God. Otherwise it is like a tanker with no fuel. That is why this book refers to positive thinking only in the context of a relationship with God. Otherwise it is as useless as every other so-called solution to worry. There is no such thing as peace unless you are willing to relate yourself properly to the Lord Jesus Christ, the Prince of Peace. Apart from that divine help, a proper mental attitude cannot be achieved and sustained. Attempt to convince yourself that you can beat worry on your own just by applying the right mental technique, and you condemn yourself to failure and frustration.

And certainly don't take "the easy way out"

The U.S. National Center for Health Statistics publication *National Vital Statistics Reports* (vol. 48, no. 11, July 24, 2000) details the ten leading causes of death in the United States in 1998. Diseases of the heart ranked number 1, with 724,859 deaths, or 268.2 deaths per 100,000 population. Suicide ranked number 8, with 30,575 deaths, or 11.3 per 100,000 population.

Thousands of people every year resort to the "solution" of suicide. Tragically, many of those who take this route have many years of potentially happy and fulfilling life ahead of them. The American Academy of Child and Adolescent Psychiatry reports that suicide is the third-leading cause of death for 15-24 year olds, and the sixth-leading cause of death for 5-15 year olds.

One of the most heartrending articles I've ever read appeared on the front page of the May 21, 1931 edition of *The New York Times*. This article dealt with the suicide of Ralph Barton. He was an outstanding cartoonist, one of the nation's best. He was highly gifted both as an artist and as a writer. Yet his life ended tragically by his own hand. In his suicide note he told about the melancholia he had been suffering. Apparently his fears nearly drove him mad. Part of the note read:

> Melancholia has prevented my getting anything like the full value out of my talent, and the past three years has made work a torture to do at all. It has made it impossible for me to enjoy the simple pleasures of life.

He goes on:

> I have run from wife to wife, from house to house, and from country to country, in a ridiculous effort to escape from myself. In doing so I am very much afraid that I have brought a great deal of unhappiness to those who have loved me. …No one thing is responsible for this, and no one person but myself… I did it because I am fed up with inventing devices for getting through the twenty-four hours a day and with bridging over a few months periodically with some beautiful interest….

Poor fellow. Brilliant of mind! How tragic that a life such as his, filled with great possibilities for blessing his generation in the will of God, had to end in such tragedy! The note traces clearly the trail of failed solutions. He could have won over worry. But he never found the way to do it.

3

THE PEACE FORMULA

A Democrat from the South asked a man living in Republican Vermont, "Why are you a Republican?"

The Vermonter answered, "My father was a Republican, and my grandfather was a Republican, and, therefore, I am a Republican."

The Southerner said, "Suppose your father had been a fool, and your grandfather had been a fool. Then what would you be?"

"Oh," the man replied, "in that case, I'd be a Democrat."

Try as you may, you cannot blame your worries on a congenital condition communicated through your genes, a condition inherited from your parents. I've heard people say, "It's just the way I am. My mother was a worrier, and my father was a worrier. So I am a worrier too. It's in the genes."

I'll be frank with you. You can't trace worry to your genes. You have not had it passed down to you from worrying parents or grandparents. You cannot excuse it as an uncontrollable state of mind. Worry is a SIN, plain and simple. It is an action you choose to do, or a condition that you permit. In either case, it can be defined as rebellion against the will of God.

Worry is a Sin

It is a sin for three reasons.

Worry is a sin because worriers distrust God

When you worry, you accuse God of falsehood:

- God's Word says, "We know that all things work together for good to them that love God, to them who are the called according to his purpose" (Romans 8:28). Yet worry says, "This is not true; God's Word cannot be trusted!"

- God's Word says, "He hath done all things well" (Mark 7:37). Yet worry says, "This is not true; God's Word cannot be trusted!"

- God's Word says, "I can do all things through Christ which strengtheneth me" (Philippians 4:13). Yet worry says, "This is not true; God's Word cannot be trusted!"

- God's Word says, "God shall supply all your need according to his riches in glory by Christ Jesus" (Philippians 4:19). Yet worry says, "This is not true; God's Word cannot be trusted!"

- God's Word says, "I will never leave thee, nor forsake thee" (Hebrews 13:5). Yet worry says, "This is not true; God's Word cannot be trusted!"

- God's Word says, "He careth for you" (1 Peter 5:7). Yet worry says, "This is not true; God's Word cannot be trusted!"

- God's Word says, "Take no thought for your life, what ye shall eat, or what ye shall drink; nor yet for your body, what ye shall put on. . . . for your heavenly Father knoweth that ye have need of all these things" (Matthew 6:25a,32b). Yet worry says, "This is not true; God's Word cannot be trusted!"

Worry wears the cloak of hypocrisy, for it professes faith in God and at the same time assails the truth of His promises. You insult a man if you call him a liar (although David probably spoke the truth when he said, "All men are liars"). How infinitely more inexcusable it is to accuse the sovereign God of falsehood! Scripture asserts that God, by His very nature, cannot deceive. As Christians, we live "in hope of eternal life, which God, that cannot lie, promised before the world began" (Titus 1:2). Consequently, "he that believeth not God hath made him a liar . . ." (1 John 5:10).

Worry is a sin because it damages the temple of God

Imagine that a group of vandals crashed into your church some dark night and shattered the stained-glass windows, ripped up the carpeting, smashed the furniture, wrecked the musical instruments, disfigured the walls, and ravaged the Sunday school rooms. What would you do?

Almost certainly, you would react with justifiable anger. If the intruders were caught, you would prosecute them to the full extent of the law, which provides stringent penalties for the disturbance of public worship and destruction of church property. Vandalism is costly, wasteful, and destructive, and we are right to condemn it.

But compare this vandalizing of a church building with what anxiety does to your bodily health. In all probability, these vandals were not professing Christians. Yet many worriers are. Furthermore, there is no eternal value in a church building. True, it symbolizes worship. It symbolizes the work and the Word of God. But the people of God do not suffer injury if a church building is destroyed. God does not dwell in the sanctuary; He dwells in the hearts of those who worship there.

> *Know ye not that ye are the temple of God, and that the Spirit of God dwelleth in you?*
> —1 CORINTHIANS 3:16

> *What? Know ye not that your body is the temple of the Holy Ghost which is in you, which ye have of God, and ye are not your own?*
> —1 CORINTHIANS 6:19

> *Ye also, as lively stones, are built up a spiritual house, a holy priesthood, to offer up spiritual sacrifices, acceptable to God by Jesus Christ.*
> —1 PETER 2:5

> *And because ye are sons, God hath sent forth the Spirit of his Son into your hearts . . .*
> —GALATIANS 4:6

If you are a Christian, remember that worry damages and even destroys the temple of God, which is your body. In Chapter 1, I mentioned the now well-established link between worry and disease. Consider again the vast range of ways in which worry impacts your physical and mental well-being. Anxiety produces heart trouble, high blood pressure, asthma, rheumatism, ulcers and other stomach disorders, colds, thyroid malfunction, arthritis, migraine headaches, blindness, palpitations, back and neck pain, indigestion, nausea, constipation, diarrhea, dizziness, fatigue, insomnia, allergies, and more. In short, worry damages your body more severely than any vandals would damage a church.

Worry is a sin because it damages relationships

When you let worry loose, it's not only your body that suffers. In all kinds of ways, worry infects and degrades your ability to relate to others. For example:

1. *Worry damages your relationship with God.* Worry is a sin because it is symptomatic of prayerlessness. "Moreover as for me, God forbid that I should sin against the LORD in ceasing to pray for you . . ." (1 Samuel 12:23). No one can pray and worry at the same time, as God tells Isaiah: "Thou wilt keep him in perfect peace, whose mind is stayed on thee: because he trusteth in thee" (Isaiah 26:3). When you pray, your mind is set on Christ, and you have His assurance of perfect peace. Worry is therefore banished.

2. *Worry damages your relationship with family.* Paul writes to the Ephesians: "Wives, submit your-selves unto your own husbands, as unto the Lord. . . . Husbands, love your wives, even as Christ also loved the church, and gave himself for it. . . . Nevertheless let every one of you in particular so love his wife even as himself; and the wife see that she reverence her husband" (Ephesians 5:22,25,33). These injunctions in the book of Ephesians are violated and disobeyed when worry sits in the saddle.

3. *Worry damages your relationship with unbelievers.* Worry is a sin because it undermines our Christian witness. In Matthew 5:16 Jesus says, "Let your light so shine before men, that they may see your

good works, and glorify your Father which is in heaven." Who would want to join a church full of worriers?

Someone may say, "Oh, yes, Dr. Haggai, it's all very well for you to talk like that in an overly confident and pedantic manner. After all, you are an ordained minister. What do you know about worry?"

Well, let me remind you of where I started. I too hold the distinction of having suffered a so-called nervous breakdown. I say "so-called" because we are mistaken if we see such crises as originating in the nervous system. Most breakdowns are not organic in nature; rather, they spring directly from the pressure of circumstances. They arise when we allow our lives to tumble out of control.

How the Bible deals with worry

The Bible is the only book that deals adequately with the problem of sin. Quite logically, then, we should go to the Word of God to find the solution to the sin of worry. I direct your attention to some of the many relevant verses of Scripture, and will let them speak for themselves.

Rejoice in the Lord always: and again I say, Rejoice. Let your moderation be known unto all men. The Lord is at hand. Be careful for nothing; but in every thing by prayer and supplication with thanksgiving let your requests be made known unto God. And the peace of God, which passeth all understanding, shall keep your hearts and minds through Christ Jesus. Finally, brethren, whatsoever things are true, whatsoever things are honest, whatsoever things are just, whatsoever things are pure, whatsoever things are lovely,

whatsoever things are of good report; if there be any
virtue, and if there be any praise, think on these things.

—PHILIPPIANS 4:4-8

J.B. Phillips translates the same passage as follows:

Delight yourselves in the Lord; yes, find your joy in
him at all times. Have a reputation for gentleness, and
never forget the nearness of your Lord. Don't worry
over anything whatever; tell God every detail of your
needs in earnest and thankful prayer, and the peace of
God, which transcends human understanding, will
keep constant guard over your hearts and minds as
they rest in Christ Jesus. My brothers I need only add
this. If you believe in goodness and if you value the
approval of God, fix your minds on whatever is true
and honorable and just and pure and lovely and
admirable.

—PHILIPPIANS 4:4-8 PHILLIPS

Now give thought to the words of our Lord in Matthew
6:25-34:

Therefore I tell you, stop being perpetually uneasy
(anxious and worried) about your life, what you shall
eat or what you shall drink; or about your body, what
you shall put on. Is not life greater [in quality] than
food, and the body [far above and more excellent] than
clothing? Look at the birds of the air; they neither sow
nor reap nor gather into barns, and yet your heavenly
Father keeps feeding them. Are you not worth much
more than they?

And who of you by worrying and being anxious can add one unit of measure (cubit) to his stature or to the span of his life? [Psalm 39:5-7]. And why should you be anxious about clothes? Consider the lilies of the field and learn thoroughly how they grow; they neither toil nor spin. Yet I tell you, even Solomon in all his magnificence (excellence, dignity and grace) was not arrayed like one of these [1 Kings 10:4-7]. But if God so clothes the grass of the field, which today is alive and green and tomorrow is tossed into the furnace, will He not much more surely clothe you, O you of little faith?

Therefore do not worry and be anxious, saying, What are we going to have to eat? or, What are we going to have to drink? or, What are we going to have to wear? For the Gentiles (heathen) wish for and crave and diligently seek all these things, and your heavenly Father knows well that you need them all. But seek (aim at and strive after) first of all His kingdom, and His righteousness (His way of doing and being right), and then all these things taken together will be given you besides. So do not worry or be anxious about tomorrow, for tomorrow will have worries and anxieties of its own. Sufficient for each day is its own trouble.

—MATTHEW 6:25-34 (AMPLIFIED BIBLE)

The peace formula

The passage in Philippians 4:4-8 constitutes the biblical basis for this book. If we look at it closely, we can discover within it the simple formula for winning over worry. I call it the Peace Formula, and it runs as follows:

PRAISE + POISE + PRAYER = PEACE

Subsequent chapters will amplify and develop this formula. For now let me only suggest that observance of the formula would sweeten the atmosphere of many homes, convert many a faltering business into a thriving success, significantly improve the scholastic level of many a student, give meaning and purpose to many an aimless life, and deliver many a person from a premature grave by curing psychosomatic illness that, if left unchecked, could become irreversible and permanent.

If you are serious about winning over your worries, write this formula down in large letters. For your convenience I have included a page with the formula on five perforated steps. You'll find this on the last page in the book. Place a copy on the mirror of your medicine cabinet where you shave, or on the mirror of your dressing table. If you work outside the home, place one in a conspicuous place in your office. If you spend your time at home, place one over the sink or on the coffee table. If you are a driver, attach one to the sun visor in your automobile. The more places you put the formula, the more you will be reminded of it, and the more deeply it will embed itself into your consciousness.

Let me further suggest that you memorize Philippians 4:4-8 and repeat the words to yourself as an affirmation every morning when you wake up. That way you will make these essential words of God a part of your very being. It won't take you long. And it will set you firmly on the road to victory.

4

Our Impelling Motive

As a child, I was small and sickly, and the prey of every bully on the school playground.

One day during holiday time in the summer of 1934, I was in Grand Rapids, Michigan, with my cousin Alex Haddad. I had accompanied him down to Seymour Square to pick up some groceries for his mother. We had nearly returned to their little house on Burton Street when three big fellows in a pickup truck came by and shouted, "Haddad, get yourself and that blankety-blank Hebrew-Wop-Dago cousin of yours out of here before we mop up the gutter with you."

Immediately I cringed. I thought to myself, *Uh-oh, here comes another beating.* Then I looked over at Alex, and my fears subsided; a peaceful calm replaced them. In fact, I started to smile. That year, Alex was the AAA wrestling champion in the 175-pound division. At 15, he was very much a man. His biceps were like cannonballs and his pectoral muscles were like marble slabs.

Strangely, Alex did not answer back. I said, "Alex, you're not going to let them get by with that, are you?"

"Well, John, you know what the Bible says: If they hit you on one cheek, turn the other."

I had never remembered Alex being that spiritual before, but I was in no position to contest his decision! So I kept walking with him toward the house. We went inside the little picket fence, and just as we got to the front door, he handed the other bag of groceries to me and said, "John, take these in to Mom. Tell her I forgot something; I'll be right back."

I knew exactly what he had forgotten. I shoved the groceries inside the front door and then trailed him back down to Seymour Square. He surmised that the three roughnecks were on their way to Miller's ice cream parlor. I got to the location just in time to watch Alex knock the biggest of the three fellows out cold and addle a second fellow with another powerful blow, while the third ran away in stark terror.

I pushed back the shoulders of my four-foot, 10-inch frame, brushed the palms of my hands together, and said to myself, "Anyone else?"

What had converted me from a terrified little boy to a calm and serene fellow brimming with confidence? A simple answer: Alex was near.

In just the same way, the Lord is near to all who profess faith in Him. "Let your moderation be known unto all men. The Lord is at hand" (Philippians 4:5).

A literal translation of Philippians 4:5b shows that the verb is missing—"the Lord near." No verb was needed. It is abrupt, staccato. It is a bolt of light. The awareness of His nearness gives great calm in the storm and stress of life.

Living in the awareness of that fact brings about a behavioral change that cannot be explained in human terms. It's often the only major difference between a defeated Christian and a victorious Christian. Fortune may have eluded you. Professional success, which you have sought so laboriously, may have slipped through your fingers. Love may have betrayed you. All these may be true.

But the Lord is near! There is no mockery in that statement. Those few words impel us to observe the mandates set down in Philippians 4:4-8.

The four kinds of nearness

The commentators of the Bible distinguish four ways in which the Lord remains near:

1. *The Lord is near in His presence*—in the same way a person in the next room is near. "Thou art near, O LORD," sang the psalmist (Psalm 119:151a). And the apostle Paul echoes and glorifies the ancient song. The Lord is near in that He indwells, by the Holy Spirit, the individual Christian. He is "Christ in you" (Colossians 1:27).

2. *The Lord is near in His availability.* The psalmist cried, "The LORD is nigh unto all them that call upon him" (Psalm 145:18). Here again the New Testament echoes the Old Testament. As children of God we have His ear because we have His heart. A distant Lord would depress us and distress us. An unapproachable Savior could not help us. Thank God, Christ is approachable. "For we have not a high priest which cannot be touched with the feeling of our infirmities; but was in all points tempted like as we are, yet without sin. Let us therefore come boldly unto the throne of grace, that we may obtain mercy, and find grace to help in time of need" (Hebrews 4:15,16).

3. *The Lord is near in His compassion.* In the exigencies and vicissitudes of life the Lord is near. The psalmist affirmed this truth when he sang, "The LORD is nigh unto them that are of a broken heart" (Psalm 34:18). Who has not known the distressful

mystery of a broken heart! "God is . . . a very present help in trouble" (Psalm 46:1). The consciousness of Christ's compassion induces poise.

4. *The Lord is near in His return.* The Lord is also at hand eschatologically. He is coming again in clouds of heaven with great glory. I believe His coming is sooner than we think—the possibility was certainly very real to the early Christians. He Himself declared it in no ambiguous terms. Jesus may come today. In the silence and darkness of midnight His trumpet may sound and His awful glory blaze upon us! Our love of His appearing is the greatest inducement to obedience. Every command laid upon us is more easily fulfilled when we are motivated by the continuous consciousness of the possibility that Jesus may come *today.* "Be ye also ready" (Matthew 24:44). Readiness for His return should make us rich in Christian character. Contemplation of this truth will make us like Him who is our great Exemplar.

God's nearness is the key to peace

As you live in the consciousness of the nearness of the Lord, you will find strength to help you to apply the biblical formula for peace:

1. *Praise.* You will find strength and inclination to excite praise, even when circumstances would drag your spirits down. Living in the consciousness of the nearness of our Lord will dispel the clouds of pessimism and lead you into the sunshine of enthusiasm and optimism. You cannot live in the consciousness of His nearness and go around looking as if you were born in crab-apple

time, put up in vinegar, and weaned on a dill pickle.

2. *Poise.* You will find poise much easier to achieve as you live in the consciousness of the nearness of your Lord. For instance, you will find that your thoughts are pleasing to God, and therefore positive—thus putting worry on the run. As you live in the consciousness of His nearness, you will realize a strength that is not your own, enabling you to exercise the self-control, establishing poise and banishing worry. "The steps of a good man are ordered by the LORD" (Psalm 37:23).

3. *Prayer.* When we pray we don't always *feel* the nearness of God. Sometimes, in difficult times, God can seem very far away. Yet the Bible reassures us that He is near: "Though I walk through the valley of the shadow of death, I will fear no evil; for thou art with me" (Psalm 23:4). It is God's Word we should listen to, not our feelings. The state of our emotions will shift from day to day and hour to hour. But God's Word remains constant and true.

To sum up: The Lord is near in His presence, His availability, His compassion, and His return. That should remind us that He is watching everything we do. It should assure us that He stands ready and eager to supply the needed resources to fulfill our every responsibility to Him and for Him. And it should motivate us to live every moment in a way that would not shame us were He to suddenly burst upon the scene.

In these three words, "the Lord near," lies a dynamic truth. These words can produce the motive power generating attitudes and activities in fulfillment of the divine demands.

Part 2

PRAISE

5

THE REQUIREMENT
TO REJOICE

Owen Cooper of Yazoo City, Mississippi, saw his house go up in smoke. He was one of the nation's outstanding Christian laymen and one of Mississippi's top-ranking citizens. Some members of the family barely escaped with their lives. The fire completely gutted the home and destroyed nearly everything of value.

Shortly after this terrible fire, Cooper's pastor, Dr. Harold Shirley, told me that the entire family attended a prayer meeting the following night. In that service Owen Cooper arose during the testimony time and, with a radiance that only God can give, expressed his gratitude to the Lord for sparing their lives. He had learned years before the truth of Romans 8:28: "We know that all things work together for good to them that love God, to them who are the called according to his purpose." Despite calamity, the habit pattern of the Cooper family could not be thrown off track.

Happiness is something you choose

When Paul wrote about happiness he did not say, "I hope you will be happy." He *told* people to be happy:

Rejoice evermore.
—1 THESSALONIANS 5:16

Rejoice in the Lord always: and again I say, Rejoice.
—PHILIPPIANS 4:4

Delight yourselves in the Lord; yes, find your joy in him at all times.
—PHILIPPIANS 4:4 PHILLIPS

You say, "But I don't feel like rejoicing. I don't feel like being happy."

By that you mean that the circumstances engulfing you are not such as contribute to your happiness. The majority of chronic worriers think of happiness as something that happens to them, like the sun coming out after a rainstorm. And so they make the mistake of being passive—waiting until their circumstances change. Of course there is nothing wrong with changing difficult circumstances yourself, if you have that option. But happiness is not a state of becoming. It is a state of *being*. You don't acquire happiness. You *assume* happiness.

I emphasize again: Philippians 4:4 is in the imperative mood. It is mandatory. Paul isn't making helpful suggestions, he's giving a command. "Rejoice in the Lord always: and again I say, Rejoice." Literally, it could be translated, "Keep on rejoicing in the Lord always: and again I say, keep on rejoicing." Make the joy of the Lord the habit pattern of your life. For when you fail to do this, you sin, and you suffer.

The key to rejoicing is praise

You rejoice when you praise. You cannot praise God without rejoicing in God and rejoicing in the circumstances —no matter how unpleasant—which God permits.

The word "praise" in its various forms, and the word "rejoice" in its various forms, are mentioned more than 550 times in the Word of God. The very fact that this subject receives such frequent attention in the Bible indicates its importance.

In Psalm 34:1, David said, "I will bless the LORD at all times: his praise shall continually be in my mouth." Praise was the habit pattern of David's life, even though, like all of us, David had many troubles and difficulties. He often passed through deep waters. One son, Adonijah, broke his heart. Absalom, another son, betrayed his father and tried to usurp his authority. Another son, Ammon, grieved David by committing adultery with his half-sister, Tamar. You also remember how viciously Shimei cursed David on one occasion. And every Sunday school pupil remembers the story of Saul's persecution of David. Saul repeatedly sought David's life and hounded him with barbaric intensity.

Yet, in all of this David blessed the Lord and fulfilled the requirement to rejoice. God's praise was continually in David's mouth.

In Psalm 33:1, David admonishes us: "Rejoice in the LORD, O ye righteous: for praise is comely for the upright." This is the injunction of the man who was "a man after God's own heart."

After the local authorities had mercilessly beaten Peter and the apostles for speaking "in the name of Jesus" the apostles departed, "rejoicing that they were counted worthy to suffer shame for his name" (Acts 5:40,41).

You are entitled to no particular commendation simply because you rejoice when everything goes well. When, however, you have made praise and rejoicing the habit pattern of your life, you have arrived at that place where you not only bring glory to God, but also set up an immunity against worry.

Rejoice even on blue Mondays and black Fridays. Though it seems that friends have betrayed you, neighbors are vicious and mean to you, relatives don't appreciate you, and tragedy overtakes you, it nevertheless remains true that you will conquer worry with the attitude expressed in Isaiah 12:2,4: "Behold, God is my salvation; I will trust, and not be afraid: for the Lord JEHOVAH is my strength and my song; he also is become my salvation. . . . And in that day shall ye say, Praise the LORD, call upon his name, declare his doings among the people, make mention that his name is exalted."

Praise is always possible

Remember what I have written earlier. There is no condition or circumstance that can justify worry. Worry is a sin. Praise is an antidote to worry.

One of the most radiant Christian men I have ever met passed through a heart-crushing trial. To help augment the family income during the depression, he and his wife provided room and board for a "highly respected citizen." The man whom they took in turned out to be a Judas, a betrayer. He seduced his host's wife with diabolical cunning. When she tried to break off the relationship he went berserk. He strangled her and then put her baby in the oven and turned on the gas, murdering the little one by asphyxiation. He then took the couple's eight-year-old son out into the garage and strangled him with a piece of wire. Finally he returned to the kitchen and lay down on some chairs in front of the stove with the gas jets wide open.

The rescue squad was able to revive the viperous murderer. But a radiant Christian man lost, in one fell swoop, his wife and children. This crushing blow would have upset the mental balance of a lesser man. Yet in the strength of the Lord he actually went to the penitentiary to witness to the murderer. The way he conducted himself through that ordeal, and during the subsequent years, has made a powerful impact on me—and on thousands of others—for good and for God.

Of course he was grief-stricken. But through it all the joy of the Lord remained his abiding and unwavering possession.

You say you have troubles? Sure you do. We all do. When rejoicing has become the habit pattern of your life you are not a thermometer personality who registers the temperature of your environment. You are rather a thermostat personality, setting the temperature of your environment. You have learned, in the words of Paul, to "rejoice evermore" (1 Thessalonians 5:16).

Paul was no "ivory-tower theorist." He urged the Christians at Philippi, "Rejoice in the Lord always: and again I say, Rejoice" (Philippians 4:4). At the time he wrote those words he was a prisoner in Rome. Almost certainly he knew Nero would never release him. He surely knew that ahead of him lay the executioner's sword. Yet he did not say, "Cry with me," or "Mourn with me," but "Rejoice with me."

If Paul could rejoice in circumstances like that, what excuse can we find for our anxieties?

6

HOW TO CONTROL YOUR FEELINGS

Norman Cousins, the famous essayist and longtime editor of the *Saturday Review,* once fell so seriously ill that doctors did not expect him to live. Cousins took stock. He concluded that if bad emotions can induce illness, good emotions should do the reverse. He determined to think and act in a cheerful, positive, and upbeat manner, on the premise that "a merry heart doeth good like a medicine." It worked. And Cousins survived to write a book about the experience, titled *Anatomy of an Illness.*

Take hold of your emotional steering wheel

It is a basic law of human nature that you will feel as you think and act. Think and act the way you want to feel—and soon you will feel the way you are thinking and acting. Ideally this will be the way God wants you to feel. Let me give you an illustration.

Go to a quiet room, stand with your feet about a foot apart at the heels, and clasp your hands behind your back, letting them hang loosely. Bow your back and neck and head slightly, maintaining complete relaxation of the body. Now start thinking resentful thoughts.

Did you observe what happened? Immediately you straightened up because of the contraction of your muscles. You became taut. Your thoughts, feelings, and actions interrelated.

When a man comes into my study and sits down in a relaxed manner, placing the ankle of his right leg loosely over the knee of his left leg, and leans back, I know he has absolute confidence in me. He has no fear of me, for a position of defense would be hard to assume from this posture.

Carry this over into your everyday life. When you are depressed and forlorn and feel that you have nothing but trouble, then smile. Throw your shoulders back. Take a good deep breath. Sing. Better still, force yourself to laugh. Keep forcing it until you are laughing heartily. At first it will seem mockery, but I guarantee you, it will chase away your gloom.

You cannot think fear and act courageously. Conversely, you cannot think courage and act fearfully. You cannot think hatred and act kindly. Conversely, you cannot think kindly and act hatefully. Your feelings inevitably correspond to your dominant thoughts and actions.

Is this scriptural? Absolutely! God's Word says, "For as he thinketh in his heart, so is he" (Proverbs 23:7).

Alfred Adler, the famous Austrian psychiatrist, who later served as visiting professor at Columbia University in New York and at the Long Island School of Medicine, taught that those who are immersed in helping others do not suffer feelings of inferiority, neuroses, or psychoses.

Indeed, financial generosity and its corollary, compassion in positive action, strengthens and even sustains the kind of poise that is otherwise impossible.

How thought and body are linked

Now once again read Philippians 4:8 and see how important it is:

> *Finally, brethren, whatsoever things are true, what-*
> *soever things are honest, whatsoever things are just,*
> *whatsoever things are pure, whatsoever things are*
> *lovely, whatsoever things are of good report; if there*
> *be any virtue, and if there be any praise, think on*
> *these things.*
>
> —PHILIPPIANS 4:8

Obedience to the command of Philippians 4:8 will result in obedience to the command of Philippians 4:4. As you think, so will you feel. Our feelings are revealed by our actions.

For instance, when I see a man with his feet set at ten minutes to two and his lips at twenty past eight, who pushes his weight instead of carrying it, I say to myself, "Watch out. This man is a potential tyrant." When I see a woman nervously moving her wedding band back and forth on her ring finger, I surmise that she and her husband are not getting along too well. I'm usually right.

No, you may not be able to directly control your feelings, but you can control your thoughts and actions. Therefore, in the strength of Christ, master your thoughts and actions and thus dominate your feelings.

It is impossible for you to "rejoice in the Lord always" and to worry at the same time. Furthermore, you cannot remove thoughts of worry and fear simply by saying, "I don't want to be afraid. I don't want to worry."

To win over worry, discipline yourself to think upon the "these things" of Philippians 4:8. Let your actions accommodate themselves to your thoughts. Discipline yourself to smile, to maintain good posture, to talk with a musical voice in a dynamic manner—in short, to act in a manner compatible with these positive thoughts.

Don't start tomorrow; start today. Start now. Your worries will flee. And God will be glorified.

Controlling thoughts and actions neutralize the divided mind

Bob Glaze of Dallas, Texas, has distinguished himself as a Bible teacher, a patron of the arts, a civic leader, a family man, and a businessman. He has been a member of the President's Council of the Dallas Symphony Association. He has taught a Bible class every Sunday morning for more than 40 years, and has been written up in such prestigious business publications as *Fortune* as an outstanding businessman.

Bob is a certified public accountant by profession. Things went very well for him from the time he was discharged from the Navy, where he served as an officer during World War II. After several years as a comptroller for a large organization, he and three friends decided to go into business for themselves. The business collapsed within a year. Bob did not panic or go into the trough of depression. He took control of his situation and, like a superb sea captain, skillfully maneuvered the ship of his life through dangerous and uncharted waters.

He would not compromise with just any position that came along. He determined what he would like to do and with whom he would like to be associated. His number-one choice was America's leading developer, Trammel Crow of Dallas.

Bob had heard that Trammel Crow was a fitness buff. So Bob got into first-class shape himself. He was 43 years old at the time. He made an appointment with Trammel Crow. During the interview, Trammel suggested they visit the fourteenth floor of one of his buildings. Bob had heard that Trammel did not take elevators but, rather, ran up the steps. When Trammel arrived at the fourteenth floor, Bob was right behind him. Later Bob chuckled as he recounted the experience and said, "I don't know if Trammel hired me because he thought I was a good man for the job or because he was impressed that I could stay with him up the 14 flights of stairs!"

The point I'm making is that Bob kept his focus so tightly on his objective that he did not permit a divided mind. He gave no room to worry at all. He controlled his feelings by controlling his thoughts and his actions. And he secured the position he wanted, to the delight of both Trammel Crow and himself.

Controlling thoughts and actions restores health

In November 1986, Bob was rushed to the hospital with a severe case of pancreatitis. His sickness and the complications from it lasted for more than seven months. The cause of the problem lay in his gall bladder. However, Bob was so weak they could not take the chance of operating. For weeks on end, he was fed intravenously. Three times, according to the doctors, they nearly lost him. After his gall bladder surgery, Bob announced to the doctors the day he would go home. They were skeptical, but Bob acted on the conviction that the surgery was a success and that he would be home earlier than the doctors had originally suggested. And he was.

This is no appeal to foolhardiness. Bob would not be imprudent. He was simply positive. Today, in later life, he is back at his usual pace, which would challenge many a younger man. Bob is quick to acknowledge that God supernaturally intervened in restoring him to health. He and his wife Ruth believe that God heard the prayers of literally thousands of Christian friends around the world. And he is quick to give God the glory, as are all of us who had a share in helping to love him and pray him through this ordeal. However, I must quickly point out that Bob, during this time, never permitted himself to focus his attention on anything except the expectation that he would survive, get well, and live a vigorous and fruitful life.

I submit to you that God honored his faith and the faith of his friends. And God also honored the focus of his mind, which gave foundation to the kinds of emotions that are helpful in healing.

Take control of your thoughts and feelings, and, I am certain, God will honor your faith too.

Kick the habit of defeatism

Much damage is done to the cause of Christ by professing Christians who shout out their defeatism and negativism by the limp manner with which they shake hands, the listless way in which they walk, the sourpuss countenance they maintain, and the plaintive and whining way in which they speak. I believe that these people do more damage to the cause of Christ than all of the bootleggers, extortionists, whoremongers, drunkards, and gutter riffraff put together.

When I was pastor of a large church in a southern city, I faced problems that would have challenged my sanity had it not been for the grace of God. One particular problem, which was kept from the congregation, came to my attention and the attention of several other church officers: one of the senior deacons was enmeshed in sin. To make matters worse, he showed no signs of remorse and/or any desire to repent. Evidence was also uncovered that another prominent member was stealing over $160 a week from the Sunday school offerings. We faced a tough dilemma. If we made either matter public, it could cause irreparable damage to the testimony of Christ.

In addition to these problems, my wife and I had a sorrow in our home. Our precious little son was totally paralyzed. He suffered from cerebral palsy as a result of birth injuries caused by an intoxicated doctor. The little fellow was hovering between life and death. Where was the answer to my despondency?

My mind was drawn to Psalm 1. As never before I learned to appreciate the wisdom of that blessed man who delights in the law of the Lord *day and night*. I did not want to feel as I was feeling. It was not a good testimony. Therefore, by God's grace I fastened my thoughts upon the "these things" of Philippians 4:8 and endeavored to act in a compatible manner. On several occasions I would get into my car, drive outside the city, and literally force myself to laugh and to sing. I'm sure some passers-by thought I was crazy. But this procedure was exactly what kept me sane!

Think and act the way God would have you to think and act. Result? You will feel as you think and act. This will glorify God. It will help you give worry the brush-off.

From bicycles to banking

Dr. Mochtar Riady, an ethnic Chinese Indonesian, always had his heart set on banking. Fifty years ago, it was not possible for ethnic Chinese to work in prestigious positions. Yet Riady never lost his focus nor weakened in his determination to some day go into the banking business.

While he was waiting, he began importing and selling bicycle spare parts. The day came when he was given a menial job in the bank. He worked fervently and faithfully. During this time he pursued his studies. He kept up this incredible pace until he earned a doctorate.

He formed the now world-famous Lippo Group of companies, including Lippo Bank and later the Lippo Life Insurance Company. He developed a multinational business that included banking, insurance, urban development, retailing, properties, healthcare, education, and the Internet.

In a period of less than three years, he and son James developed a 600-acre nondescript piece of land into a "city of tomorrow." Many global business analysts considered Lippo Karawaci the most advanced in Asia; some consider it the most advanced in the world.

Dr. Riady also made arrangements for his sons to receive the best possible academic education, as well as practical education (working in financial, insurance, and property institutions). On many occasions he laid everything on the line and exposed himself to what could have been financial disaster. Through it all, he treated people fairly and ensured that they would enjoy value-added benefits by their alliance with his businesses.

When he bought the 600 acres, he saw to it that all the people in the area were provided better homes than they had previously known, as well as employment opportunities previously denied to them.

He built a 300-bed hospital, a five-star hotel, and housing that compared favorably with the upscale residential districts of any city on earth.

His sons developed great business capabilities and demonstrated unusual acumen, coupled with superior human-relations skills.

On many occasions, Riady suffered opposition ranging from severe invectives to cruel betrayals. However, he never seemed to lose his upbeat, optimistic mindset and lifestyle manner. He controlled his feelings and thus controlled his environment. He did not allow his environment to control him.

During the troubles, and angered by what they perceived to be corruption at the top, some Indonesians unleashed their hostility on Riady. The damage to Lippo Karawaci amounted to millions of dollars. Yet I never heard of complaints from Riady. He must have suffered profound grief when some of those whom he had emancipated from poverty into self-respecting vocational status and financial security took part in vandalizing and looting the stores and factories in Lippo Karawaci.

During the 1990s, he, and especially his son James, were scandalized by politicians and pundits who accused the Riadys of guilt by association. It is a long story. The Riadys have not defended themselves; they have simply put their confidence in God and waited patiently for the truth to finally emerge. Thank God, as I write this, it is finally emerging. And those who are interested in the truth have come to realize the injustice.

When one walks into Riady's office, the most striking part of that office is the magnificent artistic portrayal of Jesus washing the disciples' feet.

When I visited him in 1997, I was struck by the quiet presence of Mrs. Riady in the corner of the office preparing her Bible study lesson.

Riady, a convert to the Lord Jesus Christ in his mature years and after verifiable success in business, demonstrates day by day the power of controlling one's feelings. He carries an emotional thermostat that sets the temperature around him—not a thermometer that merely responds to it.

7

COUNT YOUR
MANY BLESSINGS

There is a well-known story of a king who was so unhappy that he dispatched one of his men to go find a happy man. The king ordered, "When you find the happy man, purchase his shirt and bring it back to me that I might wear it and also be happy."

For years the king's emissary traveled and searched. He could not find a happy man. Finally, one day when he was walking in one of the poorer quarters of one of the poorest countries, he heard a man singing at the top of his voice. He followed the sound and found a man who was plowing a field. He asked the plowman, "Are you happy?"

The plowman replied, "I have never known a day of unhappiness."

The king's representative then told the plowman the purpose of his mission.

The plowman laughed uproariously as he replied, "Why, man, I don't have a shirt!"

Get out your calculator

If you would utilize the tonic of praise as an antidote to worry, you must develop a healthy respect and gratitude for the good things God has already given you.

When you're feeling down, you may have to "gird up the loins of your mind" and make a determined effort to focus your attention. God has lavishly bestowed blessings on you. Don't take them for granted.

Your blessings may not be material blessings, but they are real blessings, nevertheless. Actually, no man has ever found joy simply because he acquired material gain. Joy does not consist in the abundance of our material possessions; "a man's life consisteth not in the abundance of the things which he possesseth" (Luke 12:15b).

This very day, as I am writing this chapter, I have entertained as my luncheon guest Jean Baptiste Mugarura from Rwanda. This six-foot, two-inch, 35-year-old African took the Haggai Institute course in Advanced Leadership Training in Singapore in 1999. He was one of the youngest ever to be invited to the program.

Until five years ago, he served as an official in the National Bank of Rwanda (much like the Federal Reserve Bank of the United States). Then came the massacres inflicted upon the Rwandan people by rebel forces. Among those murdered by the rebels were John's fiancée and his mentor. Also, two of the mentor's three children were killed. His mentor, arguably one of the two most influential people in Rwanda, had exerted every effort to bring peace. Yet the rebels slaughtered him. More than one million in this country were killed. It was one of the century's worst bloodbaths.

John entered the dark night of the soul. These were days of deep reflection and self-examination. Yet if you could sit across the table from this radiant executive, now serving the Lord in Rwanda and influencing people across the world, you would never guess he had endured such an experience.

How do I account for it? This man understands the peace formula: PRAISE + POISE + PRAYER = PEACE. In the meantime, the Lord has given him a beautiful wife. He is now thoroughly immersed in full-time Christian work. He carries the load of two normally active leaders. And he is bringing hope and help to the devastated families of Rwanda. Without his ingrained and Spirit-motivated habit of counting his blessings, he could have shriveled up and become bitter and useless.

Consider your blessings. For how much money would you sell the health that God has given to you? How much does your wife's love mean to you? Have you ever thoroughly evaluated the value of your child's devotion? For what amount would you sell your reputation if it could be put on the open market? What premium do you put upon the eyesight God has given you? What about the capacity to hear, and to speak, and to feel, and to taste? Have you ever thought about how impoverished you would be if suddenly you were to be deprived of all your friends?

We tend to take the manifold blessings of God for granted, don't we? Start counting your blessings; your heart will overflow with gratitude and your lips with praise.

As the song reminds us:

> *I had the blues*
> *Because I had no shoes;*
> *Until upon the street*
> *I met a man who had no feet.*

Count your blessings. If it will help you, take time to periodically write out your blessings on a piece of paper. Praise God for the love of your wife, the affection of your children, your good health, the encouragement of your friends. As you exert some effort along this line, blessings by the score will come crowding into your consciousness. You will soon feel your heart singing, "Praise God from whom all blessings flow!" And you will be honoring the Lord in obeying the exhortation of Philippians 4:4, which tells us to rejoice always.

> *How precious also are thy thoughts unto me, O God! How great is the sum of them! If I should count them, they are more in number than the sand: when I awake, I am still with thee.*
>
> —PSALM 139:17,18

> *Many, O LORD my God, are thy wonderful works which thou hast done, and thy thoughts which are to us-ward: they cannot be reckoned up in order unto thee: if I would declare and speak of them, they are more than can be numbered.*
>
> —PSALM 40:5

Keep praising through disaster

Spurgeon, the great Baptist preacher of the last century, wrote of a young man who had suffered an accident in which he had broken his hip.

The hip did not heal properly and it left the man crippled. People prayed earnestly that God would restore this young man to health and strength. Shortly after the people began their intense and concerted intercession on behalf of this young man, apparent tragedy struck. The young man fell and broke his hip *again*.

What were they to make of this? It would have been completely natural for them to abandon their intercession, for the condition had clearly worsened, not improved. Fortunately, however, many of the intercessors—wise and mature Christians—saw God's hand in the entire affair.

They began praising Him and thanking Him for the blessing. Because it had been broken a second time, the hip had now set perfectly. It wasn't long until convalescence under God's leadership had done its perfect work. The young man walked with no limp whatsoever. The tragedy was a blessing in disguise.

Count your blessings! Even when things seem to go wrong, thank God and take courage. Say with the apostle Paul, "Most gladly therefore will I rather glory in my infirmities that the power of Christ may rest upon me" (2 Corinthians 12:9b).

In the last chapter I mentioned my son. In 1950, the Lord blessed us with a precious baby boy. After the disastrous circumstances of his birth, the little fellow nearly died. Though God was pleased to spare him, he was now totally paralyzed. He had a keen mind and all the inclinations and desires of a normal boy, but his body would not respond to the demands of his will. Oh, yes, it hurt—it hurt him and hurt us. However, God gave him a marvelously sweet disposition.

Was his paralysis a blessing? Yes. *Definitely* so. Between the year of his birth and the year I resigned the pastorate to go into full-time evangelism I undoubtedly buried more infants and ministered to more sick children than any man in any pastorate. God had conditioned me in a special way for a peculiar and yet blessed ministry. The life of my son was also a deep blessing within the family. There are many ways in which I could demonstrate this, but they involve experiences locked up in the cherished and secret places of my heart and open only to God and our immediate family.

Johnny died in 1975, 16 years after the first edition of *How to Win Over Worry* was published. People came from as far as 5,000 miles away to his funeral. One man who drove from a distant city said, "I never knew exactly how to express to Johnny what an inspiration he was to me. I wanted to come here, because I'm sure he's conscious of this service, and I just want him to know how much he meant to me."

Have the blessings given to us through Johnny survived the test of time? Indeed they have. Despite my thumbprint eyebrows, my deep voice, and my stern looks, children seem to gravitate to me. I believe I carry on a more profound correspondence with children than anyone outside the fields of teaching or child psychology. I can walk into a room where a baby is crying, speak a few words, and the baby stops crying. That I consider to be a blessing, and I must count it.

I must also count it a blessing that Christine and I have survived 55 years of marriage. The reason I say "survive" is that invalidism in the home does not bring you together; it drives you apart. Elizabeth B. Brown, wife of the celebrated medical doctor Paul Brown of Tennessee, writes of their having a sick child in the home for five years. She marvels that the two of them were able to manage it and survive the stress. According to William G. Justice, who wrote *When Death Comes* in 1982, "Ninety percent of all couples who have lost a child to death have serious marital problems within months of the death of their child. Three out of four divorce within two years."

Praise works in the toughest places

In a nation on the Pacific Rim, a young minister of the gospel preaches to between 1,200 and 1,500 people every Sunday. In that same nation, people have been slaughtered by the thousands. When I met with this remarkable leader in a neutral capital of the world, I said, "How do you handle the pressure of trying to maintain a ministry in a city and nation vocally committed to the destruction of Christianity?"

He smiled at me and said, "How good is God. What blessings He bestows!"

I thought to myself, *This poor fellow didn't hear what I said*.

But then the minister went on to explain.

"God has put us in the eye of the storm. On one side are the communists. On the other side are the Muslims. They are in such hostile combat with each other that by being in the center we are wonderfully protected. Better still, hundreds are coming to know Christ as Savior."

This man was not bemoaning his lot; he was counting his blessings. I don't think that worry finds him a suitable host.

During my visits to Vietnam in the late 1960s and early 1970s, I met with many Vietnamese people. One man stands out. He told me how he regretted the war and how sorry he was that it was necessary for American boys to come and suffer separation from home, physical injury, and even death.

Then he said, "The greatest victory of this conflict is that the Americans and the Koreans brought the gospel to our village, and we who were in darkness came to know Jesus Christ." This man had lost members of his family. He had lost his business. His home had been burned to the ground. He knew how to count his blessings!

During the Korean conflict of 1950-53, Presbyterian missionary Dr. Harold Voekel had a penetrating and pervasive ministry among the troops on both sides. He personally won to faith in Christ more than 150 North Korean soldiers, 20 of whom are now in full-time gospel ministry.

It was Voekel who introduced my mother and father, so I have more than a casual appreciation for that gentleman. The characteristic that captured my attention every time I met him was his buoyant and resilient Christian optimism in any situation. He knew how to count his blessings, and worry never seemed to catch up with him.

> *Count your blessings, name them one by one;*
> *And it will surprise you what the Lord has done.*

And one of the greatest surprises will be the fact that you are no longer saddled by that monster, worry, who has been riding hard on you.

Let me urge again that when you become depressed and worried you should take a piece of paper and literally force yourself to write out every blessing that comes to mind. Concentrate. Think hard. Sure, it will take time, but not as much time as worrying will. It won't take as much time as an interview at the psychiatrist's office—and it will be considerably cheaper. Furthermore, in the strength of God you will be actively doing something about your own condition. This is much more effective than passively submitting to psychotherapy.

I'm not saying that psychotherapy has no place, or that severer psychiatric conditions do not need a specialist's attention. Psychiatrists and counselors can provide enormous help in the right situation. Nevertheless, there are many people who frequent the offices of psychiatrists and counselors who could be enjoying full mental and emotional health right now had they only taken certain precautions and observed the biblical formula earlier in life: *Praise plus Poise plus Prayer equals Peace.* It works.

8

MASTER THE ART
OF ALTRUISM

A young college man sought counseling from Dr. George W. Truett, who was the pastor of First Baptist Church of Dallas, Texas, at that time. The student had passed through troubled waters. He said he was ready to give up his faith and that he had lost all confidence in God and people.

Dr. Truett listened to this young man. When the student finished his tale of woe, the wise and patient pastor asked the young man for a favor. The young man agreed. Dr. Truett then gave the young man the name of a hospital and the room number of a patient who was in need of a visit. Said the great-hearted minister, "I just don't have time to make the visit. You make it for me." The young man assented.

He came away from that hospital a new man. As a favor to the mighty pastor in Dallas, the young man determined to do his best. He did so well that he became genuinely interested in the patient. In so doing, his own difficulties and despair were dispelled.

In 1981, I returned to the lovely island of Bali in Indonesia. Since rooms were tight, I did not stay at my usual stopping place, the Bali Intercontinental, but instead secured accommodations at the Bali Hyatt. When I arrived and started up the steps to the entrance, several of the hotel personnel said, "Welcome to the Bali Hyatt, Dr. Haggai. Michael, our general manager, has reserved for you the best suite in the hotel. You are his guest, and you won't pay for anything."

I expressed amazement. At the registration desk to check in, one of the general manager's assistants said, "Oh, no, that is already taken care of. Let me escort you to your room." It was one of the most elegant suites I have ever seen in all of my world travels.

Within minutes, the general manager, Michael, came to my suite. I tried to express my thanks.

"You don't remember me, do you?" he said.

"No, and I apologize."

He said, "In the 1960s when you stayed at the Singapore Intercontinental, I was a bellman, hustling bags. Every time you came, you treated me just as grandly as you treated your friend, the general manager, George Milne. I have harbored a secret dream for all these years that someday I would be in charge of my own hotel and be able to show you my gratitude for the encouragement and inspiration you gave me."

That same year at Brisbane Airport, ready to board a plane headed for Sydney, I heard an announcement over the loudspeaker that the flight had been cancelled due to bad weather conditions. The passengers vented their anger on that poor Ansett Airways agent in a way I've rarely heard. I watched the way he handled them. When things quieted down and most of them had left, I walked up to him and said, "Congratulations on the masterful way you handled a situation over which you had no control. You will be the winner, believe me." He thanked me warmly, and I went back to the hotel.

A year and a half later, I was at the same airport with a coach ticket for Sydney. One of the lady agents came up to me and said, "Aren't you Dr. Haggai?"

"Yes, I am."

"Would you come this way, please?"

I followed her and was astonished when she said, "I need your ticket. We are replacing it with a first-class ticket, our compliments."

When I expressed surprise, she said, "Our manager said that last year, when people were so angry that at one point he wondered if they were going to do him bodily harm, you were the one person that kept cool and even encouraged him. This is his way–and our way–of thanking you."

If you would conquer worry with this weapon of praise you must master the art of altruism. Become genuinely interested in other people. Love your neighbor as yourself. Honor God by losing your life in serving others. By "others" I am referring not only to your employer or your family, but also to all those whom God gives you the privilege of serving.

Take the initiative

Uncle Joe Hawk was one of the most radiant personalities I have ever met. For more than half a century he was a member of the First Baptist Church of Cleveland, Tennessee. When I met him, he was 87 years old—but younger than many 25-year-olds. He attended every service I conducted in that good church in 1953.

Let me tell you a little about him, and you will catch an insight into his sparkling vitality as an octogenarian. Years before, during the Great Depression, the First Baptist Church of Cleveland, Tennessee, was in straitened circumstances. Uncle Joe Hawk was a drayman. He had been blessed with a good business, but of course he was suffering just like other businessmen during those hard years. Nevertheless, this dear man continued to put first his concern for that church and its people, many of whom had not yet accepted Christ.

At considerable personal risk, Uncle Joe sold his two finest dray horses. He gave the money to the church. Because of his gift, the First Baptist Church of Cleveland, Tennessee, stands as a mighty citadel for Christ today. Few people knew what he did. He did it without fanfare. In fact, many of the church members today are unaware of this tremendous sacrifice. Uncle Joe never got the money back from the church. He didn't expect to. He didn't want it. He gave it for the sheer joy of giving. He gave it to the eternal glory of God and for the spiritual profit of man. No man who is that interested in others has time to worry about his own problems.

When was the last time you sacrificed and sent anonymously a gift of $50 over and above your tithe to a college or seminary student who was having a hard time? When was the last time you gave something to someone anonymously—a gesture that could in no way profit you from a material standpoint?

You may say you have no money. But you don't need vast reserves of cash to be generous to others. For example:

- Perhaps the mother next door is sick and in great need of help. Why not offer to take care of the children for a couple of days? True, they may be little monsters. But that is what makes your help so valuable to their mother.

- When your neighbor goes on vacation, why not offer to take care of the mail and send it on?

- Why not drop a line of appreciation to that teacher who has taken such an interest in your child and has made such a distinct contribution to his or her highest good?

- Drop a line of gratitude to your pastor for the message that was such a blessing to you. Encourage him. It will take only a few moments of time. If you send your note by e-mail it won't even cost you a stamp.

Does not the Word of God tell us we are to esteem others better than ourselves? "Let nothing be done through strife or vainglory; but in lowliness of mind let each esteem other better than themselves" (Philippians 2:3).

Let me earnestly suggest that you determine to do something specific for someone every day—something for which no remuneration of any kind will be sought or expected. What use is morality if it isn't proactive? And besides, doing this will relieve you of the time you normally give to worrying. Your cup will run over with the joy of the Lord.

Go ahead, do it now. If it doesn't come to you easily and if you don't know how to begin, simply sit down and ask the Lord to guide you. With pencil and paper in hand, write down some things that come to your mind.

Perhaps the Lord will lead you to do the washing for the lady next door who has been hampered by her day-and-night care of sick children. Perhaps you will contact the head of some fine Christian college or seminary to secure the name of a student who is in great need. You may be led to invite a lonely church member to have dinner with you on Sunday. With just a little thought you will be able to come up with many more suggestions than these. Just go do it!

Putting yourself out for others is like a healthy diet

I am persuaded that my mother, who suffered major illnesses for the last 45 years of her life, lived to such a great age and with such great satisfaction because she immersed herself in serving others.

When a family moved into the neighborhood, she would be there with some warm food while they were getting settled. When someone was sick, she would take a card to them, as well as some thoughtful little present. She maintained correspondence with hundreds of people around the world.

I think that serving others created in her a greater capacity to praise. She was a mild-mannered lady, quiet of demeanor, but a person of strong will and great capacity to care for others.

To this day, nearly a decade after her final illness and death, people all over the world still talk to me about her. They will tell me of some little act of kindness that she had shown toward them. They will produce a postcard, a letter, or a greeting card that she had mailed to them.

One of her close friends died in 1939 in Massachusetts. Mother maintained contact with the four daughters, their spouses, and the grandchildren from 1945, when she left Massachusetts, until late 1978, when she became bedridden.

It is giving, not getting, that induces praise. It is serving, not being served, that develops the highest type of rejoicing. And, of course, no one can rejoice and worry at the same time. The two are mutually exclusive.

If you want to find real joy in living and a genuine escape from worrying, get involved in helping others. It will leave you no time to worry.

Life offers countless opportunities for altruism

A friend of mine, Elmer G. Leterman, visited Honolulu in 1935. In those days, the main mode of travel from the East Coast of the United States to Hawaii was by ship. Elmer Leterman descended the gangplank and was greeted effusively by friends who put leis around his and his wife's necks. But he noticed there were hundreds of people disembarking whom nobody met. They were not given leis. He had hardly unpacked his suitcase at the hotel before he determined that as long as he was in Hawaii, he would meet every boat with a sufficient number of leis to welcome every person who did not have someone meeting him, and put a lei around that person's neck with the robust "aloha" for which Hawaiian hospitality is internationally known.

As it turned out, people whom he contacted in this way gave him multiplied millions of dollars of business over the next 40 years, even though that was the last thing on his mind. Elmer was a happy man, always upbeat. He had mastered the art of altruism. And it left no room for a divided mind.

The late Ee Peng Liang of Singapore was a man who had earned the respect not only of the Singapore people, but of people around the world who had watched his humanitarian efforts over the years. He was a chartered accountant by profession and headed up a substantial business in Singapore.

The man never ceased to amaze me in his capacity for remembering detail. I met him once. Periodically I would get a note from him with a warm greeting. There was absolutely nothing that I could do for him in a business or personal way except give him the assurance of the continuity of my friendship and respect. But Ee Peng Liang did not do what he did in order to get things from others. He had mastered the art of altruism and impressed me as being one of the most worry-free men I have met in the course of my travels.

Help those who need help in ways they really need it

By all means, use common sense in your efforts to assist other people. Don't be like a certain young Cub Scout who had his own ideas on the subject. One night during a pack meeting the scoutmaster asked all those who had done their good deed for the day to lift their hands. All hands were lifted except the hand of one scout.

The scoutmaster barked out, "Jimmy, go out and do your good deed for the day and don't come back until you have done it."

Jimmy was gone about 20 minutes. He came back. His clothes were in shreds. His hair was disheveled. His face was cut and bleeding.

The scoutmaster said, "Jimmy, what have you been doing?"

The boy replied, "I did my good deed for the day, sir."

"What was that?" asked the scoutmaster.

"I helped an old lady across the street, sir."

"Well," said the scoutmaster, "how on earth did you get in that condition?"

"She didn't want to go," replied Jimmy.

Use common sense in your effort to help others. During the darkest part of the Depression a needy family was given an expensive pedigreed French poodle. Doubtless there is much good to be said about a French poodle. But the friend who gave the dog would have been much wiser and more helpful if she had taken the same money and purchased needed clothing and food for the family.

Assist the other person at the point of his greatest need. While doing so, remember, "It is more blessed to give than to receive" (Acts 20:35).

Kindness kills worry every time

Your genuine interest in other people will assassinate the monster of worry. Your positive thoughts of concern for others will crowd out negative fear-producing anxiety.

Reflect once again upon the concern our Lord showed for others. Even while dying, He cried out, "Father, forgive them; for they know not what they do" (Luke 23:34). And, while in the agonizing process of being executed upon the cross, He showed concern for His mother and made the finest possible preparation for her after His departure.

Real Christian discipline in the strength of God is required to master the art of altruism, but the rewards are immeasurable—especially as they relate to the altruist. Without exception, the people who are always rejoicing are people who have mastered this art of altruism, of being genuinely interested in others. This rejoicing chases away gloom and kills worry.

You will "rejoice in the Lord always" as you faithfully fulfill the injunction in Galatians 6:2-4: "Bear ye one another's burdens, and so fulfill the law of Christ. For if a man think himself to be something, when he is nothing, he deceiveth himself. But let every man prove his own work, and then shall he have *rejoicing* in himself alone, and not in another."

I share with you these same verses from the Amplified New Testament:

> Bear (endure, carry) one another's burdens and trou-
> blesome moral faults, and in this way fulfill and
> observe perfectly the law of Christ (the Messiah) and

complete what is lacking [in your obedience to it]. For if any person thinks himself to be somebody [too important to condescend to shoulder another's load] when he is nobody [of superiority except in his own estimation], he deceives and deludes and cheats himself. But let every person carefully scrutinize and examine and test his own conduct and his own work. He can then have the personal satisfaction and joy of doing something commendable [in itself alone] without [resorting to] boastful comparison with his neighbor.

—GALATIANS 6:2-4

9
DON'T EXPECT THANKS

Illustrating a sermon, Dr. R. A. Torrey once told a story he'd heard about a shipwreck in Lake Michigan. A powerful swimmer, he recalled, who was then a student at Northwestern University, had rescued 23 people as the ship went down.

To Dr. Torrey's astonishment, an elderly man at the back of the hall raised his hand.

"I was that man," he said.

Dr. Torrey asked him what stood out most in his memory about that experience after all the intervening years.

The rescuer lowered his eyes, and in a quiet voice replied, "Not a one said thanks."

Don't expect to be appreciated. When you are appreciated it will be like the cherry on top of the whipped cream of your strawberry sundae—something a little special. But don't let your rejoicing be *dependent* upon appreciation shown to you.

Our Lord healed ten lepers. Do you remember how many came back to thank Him? That's right. One!

The late General Harry C. Trexler, a wealthy philanthropist and outstanding citizen of Allentown, Pennsylvania, provided for the financial needs of 40 college students in 1933—the year in which he died. Four months before his death he called his secretary in and inquired how many young men and women he was sending through college. She told him. With mixed bewilderment and grief he replied, "And last Christmas I got only one or two Christmas cards from this group."

Some time ago, I read about a man in New York who, over a period of more than four decades, helped more than 5,000 young people secure positions in New York City. Recalling it later, he observed that only six had expressed gratitude.

The lesson? Expect ingratitude. Be generous for the joy of generosity—not to receive thanks. Give for the joy of giving, and soon you will be so thrillingly occupied with the privilege of giving that you will not have time to reflect upon the ingratitude of the recipients.

Ingratitude is the human condition

It is quite evident as you read the Pauline epistles that some of the very people whom Paul won to faith in Jesus Christ turned upon him and reviled him maliciously.

Do you know what is the basic sin? Someone answers, "Unbelief." But this is incorrect. If you will read Romans 1:21, you will conclude that ingratitude is at the root of all sin—whether that ingratitude be active or passive: "Because that, when they knew God, they glorified him not as God, neither were thankful; but became vain in their imaginations, and their foolish heart was darkened" (Romans 1:21).

Was not ingratitude the root of the sin committed by Adam and Eve?

Consider it. The Lord Jesus Christ died for us "while we were yet sinners" (Romans 5:8). He suffered. He bled.

He died—for us. Yet there are millions who, knowing this, refuse to accept Him as Savior and Lord. Why? Ingratitude!

Have you ever read about Aristotle's ideal man? Here is the philosopher's definition of him: "The ideal man takes joy in doing favors for others; but he feels ashamed to have others do favors for him. For it is a mark of superiority to confer a kindness; but it is a mark of inferiority to receive it."

Paul reminded the Christians to whom he was speaking that "it is more blessed to give than to receive" (Acts 20:35). Therefore, let your joy arise out of the blessedness of giving, of helping, of doing. Not expecting gratitude, find your joy in the very act of service.

Years ago, Samuel Johnson said, "Gratitude is a fruit of great cultivation. You do not find it among gross people."

People just don't make the effort

Remember those times when your friends have moved away to a distant location? No doubt you waxed eloquent and emotional about how you'd stay in touch, write, phone, e-mail, and visit. Think back and ask yourself how often such resolutions were actually carried out—whether it was with your gang at the college dorm, your buddies in the military service, your neighbors down the street, the friends you met on a six-day cruise overseas, your coworkers at the office or factory, or whatever.

It's not that we intend to ignore our friends. It's the apathy within us that does the work. Unless you, yourself, take measures to counteract that apathy, you'll lose the benefit of continuing relationships and uplifting experiences. But when you have examined your own heart, you'll not find it so difficult to grasp why others are also apathetic.

Take the matter of class reunions. Usually there are one or two spark plugs in the class. Were it not for them, no reunions would happen. They are the ones that take action, aggressively contact all the other members, and take steps to bring about a completely delightful experience of getting together after years of absence from each other.

It was the sage who said, "He who would have friends must show himself friendly." And maintaining friendships takes discipline, time, and energy.

To the degree that you understand the natural inclination toward apathy in your own life and grasp the insight regarding those whom you feel should not be apathetic to you, to that degree you will increase your capacity for the component of praise, the deterrent to worry and its divided mind.

I have talked many times about ingratitude to the president of Haggai Institute, Dr. William M. "Bill" Hinson, who earned his doctorate in behavioral modification. We have noted how, when you go out of your way to assist somebody, that person often seems to resent you. It's almost as if they're saying, "I could have made it on my own. I do not need you." This used to sting me.

I remember sitting in a Howard Johnson's in a Florida city one morning, when a young minister in his early thirties wept unashamedly in frustration over the church he was pastoring. He said, "For the Lord's sake, get me out of here." Then he suggested a church that he would like to pastor.

Long-term friend E. Harold Keown, Sr. and I immediately went into action. We knew that the Lord would have to open the door, but we were going to do everything possible to remove any obstructions. After a significant expenditure of our time and even money, the church called the young man. He has never said, "Thank you." He has never acknowledged that we did anything to help him. In fact, he has snubbed both of us. He is a good man, an outstanding speaker, and he has developed into a superior leader. Gratitude, however, does not seem to be high on his scale of personality characteristics.

Anticipate apathy. A young dentist in our city phoned me out of desperation one night to tell me his wife was on the threshold of suicide. I immediately made time to see this very attractive and capable young couple. We prayed together. The Lord spared her. Shortly thereafter, not only did he never say thank you, he became critical of the very work in which I am involved.

Saul never showed a genuine gratitude to David. David saved his life. David saved his kingdom. Yet Saul, jealous of David, tried to kill him on more than one occasion. Don't be surprised if you are not appreciated.

How many parents I know—friends of mine—who have immersed their children in material benefits, only to find that the children don't seem to appreciate it. The parents ask me why.

I have said to fathers who started with nothing and struggled to get where they are, "Where would you be today if your father had done for you what you have done for your children?" In each case, they either blanched or said something like, "Whew, I never thought of that." I am convinced that drowning children with material blessings risks producing ingratitude that will plague them throughout life.

The famous international investor Sir John Templeton warns that in giving great wealth to our children we run the risk of breeding pride in them. They did not earn their money. Consequently, they will always wonder if they could have made it without the largesse handed to them. One young man said, "I'm a self-made man." I replied, "If you didn't share your father's name, do you think the bank would have made you the loans you have taken out? They loaned you millions of dollars without sufficient collateral simply because you are your father's son!"

Ingratitude is a universal sin. Expect it. Give for the joy of giving. Do for the joy of doing. Help only for the joy of helping. And you won't have time even to notice the prevalence of the sin of ingratitude. Praise should be the habit pattern of your life—regardless of the cold and even cruel treatment received from some whom you have helped.

Part 3

POISE

10

POISE THROUGH
THOUGHT-CONTROL

In my first pastorate a young lady, 29 years of age, wore a facial expression that reminded me of an approaching cyclone. It came as no surprise to me to discover that she enjoyed very poor health! Her house was a mess, and her general appearance looked like an accident going somewhere to happen. When I shook her hand at the end of the service, it was so limp I felt like handing it back to her. I would say, "How are you?" She then proceeded to tell me her tale of woe.

I was only 22 years old, but I learned one lesson in a hurry. I stopped asking her how she was. When I shook her hand, *I shook* it, believe me! I gave her my finest smile and said, calling her by name, "You look so much better. You must be feeling better." Believe it or not, within a few months she was looking better and apparently feeling better. With the help of some friends, I dropped a seed thought into her mind that became a dominant thought. And as she thought, so she became.

What is poise?

Over time, what I observed in that woman was an increase in her poise. You will find poise complex in its makeup. The Amplified New Testament translates Philippians 4:5 as follows: "Let all men know and perceive and recognize your unselfishness (your considerateness, your forbearing spirit). The Lord is near [He is coming soon]."

The word translated "unselfishness," "considerateness," and "forbearing spirit" can also be rendered as "fairness," "reasonableness," "mildness," "patience," and "leniency." The word further carries the sense of "congeniality of spirit." It is all this that underlies and defines the term *poise*. You will mark the person of poise one of unassuming assurance, an easy dignity of manner. You may define poise as the peace of God expressed in human behavior.

How do we develop poise? There are many ways. But you will not get far unless you can take command of your own mental processes. Poise, then, first requires that we exercise thought control.

Control your thoughts, control your feelings

> *Finally, brethren, whatsoever things are true, whatsoever things are honest, whatsoever things are just, whatsoever things are pure, whatsoever things are lovely, whatsoever things are of good report; if there be any virtue, and if there be any praise, think on these things.*
>
> —PHILIPPIANS 4:8

> *For as he thinketh in his heart, so is he: Eat and drink, saith he to thee; but his heart is not with thee.*
>
> —PROVERBS 23:7

I have already said that while we cannot control our feelings directly, we can control them indirectly by controlling our thoughts.

You can control your thoughts consciously if you want to. To be sure, it will take some discipline. Arnold Bennett, in his splendid book *How to Live on Twenty-Four Hours a Day*, challenges the reader to think on any given subject every day for at least 15 minutes without permitting his mind to wander. I challenge you to try it.

Many people can brood for 15 minutes. They can worry for 15 minutes. But very few people can focus their attention on any given (and I might add, worthwhile) subject for 15 minutes. Almost without exception, after two minutes their minds will have drifted onto something else.

To repeat a statement previously made in this book: you cannot have thoughts of fear and, at the same time, act courageous. If you want victory over anxiety, you must develop the control of your thoughts. Only by doing this can you develop the poise that conquers worry.

We are what we think

The old saying is true. In the words of Marcus Aurelius, "A man's life is what his thoughts make of it." Ralph Waldo Emerson states that truth in another way when he says, "A man is what he thinks about all day long." Our dominant thoughts tend to externalize themselves. What lives within sooner or later finds concrete expression.

It's an old trick, but school children still love to play it. One will go to Billy and say, "You look terrible. Are you feeling well today?" A little later another one will approach him with a similar suggestion. And then a third. And a fourth. Soon the thought of his not being well becomes Billy's dominant thought—and he goes home sick!

So take care what you let into your mind. Paul instructs us to think on things that are true. Don't think on falsehood. If you think on falsehood, soon you will become false. Your heart will condemn you and your worries will increase.

Think on things that are honest and praiseworthy. As you do so, your thoughts will inevitably begin to externalize themselves. Think honestly, and you will live honestly. If you cannot describe something as good and honorable, then refuse to think of it at all. It will only pollute your mind and sap your resolve to win over your worries. Think on things that are pure. As Peter would say, "Gird up the loins of your mind" (1 Peter 1:13a). An impure thought always precedes an impure deed. Keep your thoughts pure, and your deeds will be pure. Pure thoughts are incompatible with worry thoughts.

The apostle Paul says, "Think on things of good report" (see Philippians 4:8). The words "good report" come from two words meaning "fair speaking." The phrase could also be translated "attractive." Attractive thoughts will also deliver you from worry and from being a sourpuss.

Paul then adds, "If there be any virtue, and if there be any praise, think on these things." The word "virtue" comes from the Greek word *aresko*, which means "to please." Here again, learn to control your thoughts so they will relate to that which pleases. That means they will be pleasing thoughts.

Under God, you have the power to control your thoughts. Some people unwittingly invite misery because they invite into their minds destructive thoughts. They use no discernment in the selection of the guests they invite into their minds. They think worry thoughts, fear thoughts, anxiety thoughts. Consequently they don't see the glass half full; rather, they always see it half empty. They spurn the sunlight of optimism for the ominous clouds of pessimism. They come up with sanctimonious witticisms like

"I expect the worst so I will never be disappointed." In a way they're right. Expect the worst, and you will get the worst. Thoughts of the worst dominating your life tend to externalize themselves into your outward actions, which means that your expectations become a self-fulfilling prophecy. You yourself, therefore, create a self-destroying monster.

Think for yourself

Do your own thinking. You must guard yourself even against the well-meaning but often negative and damaging advice of relatives and friends. They may mean well, but they often pull against your best interests by encouraging you to go easy on yourself. Don't leave your mind open to the negative influence of other people. Read the biography of any dynamic personality—any achiever—and almost without exception you will discover that discouraging remarks, poor advice, negative influences, and downright opposition were thrown across his or her path by people in his or her inner circle.

Misery loves company, and you can be sure that other worriers will do their best to drag you down to their level. The following story illustrates the point well.

There were two farmers. One was a pessimist, the other was an optimist.

The optimist would say, "Wonderful sunshine."

The pessimist would respond, "Yeah, I'm afraid it's going to scorch the crops."

The optimist would say, "Fine rain."

The pessimist would respond, "Yeah, I'm afraid we are going to have a flood."

One day the optimist said to the pessimist, "Have you seen my new bird dog? He's the finest money can buy."

The pessimist said, "You mean that mutt I saw penned up behind your house? He don't look like much to me."

The optimist said, "How about going hunting with me tomorrow?"

The pessimist agreed. They went. They shot some ducks. The ducks landed on the pond. The optimist ordered his dog to get the ducks. The dog obediently responded. Instead of swimming in the water after the ducks, the dog walked on top of the water, retrieved the ducks, and walked back on top of the water.

The optimist turned to the pessimist and said, "Now, what do you think of that?"

Whereupon the pessimist replied, "Hmmm, he can't swim, can he?"

In the strength of God, control your thoughts. Let them be regulated according to the will of God. Such thoughts will lead to inner poise that is a shield against worry.

11

POISE THROUGH
SELF-CONTROL

Fifty years ago, I was invited to pastor a church of 3,000 members, which at that time was considered a large church. During the first year, I took measures to add individuals to my staff, including an associate minister who seemed eminently qualified.

One day, during a private meeting in my office, I made a statement which, for the life of me, I cannot recall at the moment. I was seated behind my desk and he had sat down on the divan against the far wall. He misunderstood what I was saying, and took it as a personal insult. He glowered as he warned me, "You know, I'm a former prize fighter, and if you take this kind of an approach, I'll be forced to mop up the gutter with you."

Well, that flew all over me. I could feel the blood leaving my face. I arose slowly from my chair, moved with measured and slow tread around the desk over to where he sat, grabbed him by his shirt and tie, and raised him to his feet (he was a much bigger man than I). With my index finger I started poking his sternum as I said, "Throw the first punch, and your mother will be sorry she ever brought you into this world."

It was puerile. It was God-dishonoring. It was inexcusable. He was wrong in what he concluded and what he said. I was inexcusably wrong in my response.

His face blanched. I am sure that with his size and his experience, he could have whipped me, but at that time, neither he nor I believed it.

The next morning when I arrived at the office, I asked for him. I had endured a sleepless night. I wanted to apologize and ask his forgiveness. He had not shown up. After some investigation, I found that he had left town at midnight with his family and had left instructions for a moving company to pack up his things and send them to a location that they would not divulge to me.

Three years passed by. In the meantime, every time I reflected upon that experience, I grew sick inside. I knew that if I had many repetitions of that experience, I could drop dead of a massive stroke or a heart attack. The cardiovascular system simply could not tolerate the damage I was inflicting upon it. (Incidentally, two of my good friends—men of senior status and great business achievements—dropped dead in the midst of such explosions of anger.)

Three years later, after I had moved to another city, my executive assistant said, "Reverend So-and-so has phoned to see if you will accept a call from him." I said, "Of course. I've been trying to find him."

In a few hours, the call came through and my former assistant said, "I need to say something."

I interrupted him and said, "No, I must say something, and I must say it before you say a word." I then apologized to him in as complete and contrite and God-honoring a manner as I knew how. I asked for his forgiveness. I told him that the Lord had forgiven me, and I wanted his forgiveness.

It was a beautiful meeting by long-distance phone.

Since that time, my desire to honor the Lord and my passion for self-preservation have combined to throttle any tendency to explode. During the last half a century hence, I have become annoyed and irritated, but never angry like I experienced on that occasion and on some occasions before it.

Had the Lord not given me victory in controlling my emotions, I believe that I would not only have disgraced the Lord, but I would have long since been dead.

Never make the mistake of retaliating

Never retaliate when others hurt you. In retaliating you may force them to pay the price of their behavior toward you, but the cost to you will be far greater. The Bible tells us that we must love our enemies (see Matthew 5:44). As long as you go on hating your enemies you are giving them the sovereignty of your own life. You are literally forcing them to dominate you.

For instance, imagine there is a man who has wronged you. You loathe him. Your loathing becomes a festering personality sore. You so detest him you would not welcome him into your home. You would not permit him to fraternize with your relatives. You would not invite him to eat at your table or spend the night in your guest room. Yet, all the time you are busy hating him, you are already "entertaining" him in your bloodstream, in your brain cells, in your nerve fibers, in your muscles, and in the marrow of your bones. You are giving him power over your sleep, power over your blood pressure, power over your health, power over your happiness. You are insisting that he destroy your body and disintegrate your effectiveness. What on earth is the good of that?

Some years ago *Life* magazine carried an article on high blood pressure. In that article the statement was made that the chief personality trait of people with high blood pressure is resentment. What a price to pay for lack of self-control! The sufferers are paying financially in doctors' bills and medical assistance. They are paying emotionally with shattered nerves. They are paying in reduced efficiency, resulting in decreased income. They are paying domestically in strife with family members on whom they project their bitterness and misery. What a price!

Learn a lesson from our Lord, in whose steps we are commanded to follow: "Who, when he was reviled, reviled not again; when he suffered, he threatened not; but committed himself to him that judgeth righteously" (1 Peter 2:23). Well did the wise Solomon say, "Better . . . [is] he that ruleth his spirit than he that taketh a city" (Proverbs 16:32b).

Reflect for a moment upon the poise of the great Abraham Lincoln. In the anguish of his most grief-producing hours, he exercised poise. Had it not been for this quality it is doubtful that the Civil War would have ended in victory for the Union Army. It is highly doubtful his name would have been immortalized had it not been for his magnificent ability to retain poise and stay calm. Men in his own cabinet were disloyal to him, trying on several occasions to discredit his name. To his back they made light of him, scoffed at his limited education, and sneered at his rustic ways. Realizing that their disloyalty was to him personally, and realizing further that they possessed qualities making them essential to our nation, the ex-railsplitter exercised self-control, disregarding the insults his colleagues heaped upon him.

Practice self-control in the face of criticism

In attaining the mastery of self-control you must learn how to conquer criticism. I do not mean that you should try to avoid criticism; you will find that impossible. Nor do I mean that you should subdue criticism—that will prove counterproductive. You can conquer it, however, by treating it in the right way.

Once again, follow the example of our Lord, who answered His critics so often with silence. Our Lord defended other people. He defended the Word of God. He defended the work of His heavenly Father. He defended little children. *Yet He never defended Himself!*

Usually you will find it wise not to answer your critics, tempting though it may be to do so. "Answer not a fool according to his folly, lest thou also be like unto him" (Proverbs 26:4).

Ask yourself what answering criticism will achieve. Your friends don't need an answer, because you retain their confidence. Instead, listen to the criticism objectively. Don't allow yourself to become emotionally involved. Sometimes you can profit from the criticism. If the criticism is just, do something about it. If the criticism is unjust, ignore it.

On the other hand, if your enemies criticize you, so what? That's what enemies do. And remember that unjust criticism is often a backhanded compliment. It often indicates that you have excited the interest, jealousy, and envy of the critic. As the old adage goes, "No one ever kicks a dead dog."

Wise words from my father

My father gave me a formula for handling criticism which I have found helpful.

He said, "John, when somebody blows up at you, listen calmly and with a smile on your face. When they finish say, 'Is that all?' They will doubtlessly erupt again, but not as long nor as heatedly as before. When they are done, once again ask, 'Is that all?' Keep doing this until finally they have nothing more to say. With exasperation they may say, 'Well, is that not enough?' At that point, with calmness and still with a smile, pull the arrow out of your quiver that most succinctly and powerfully squelches the criticism. You will have retained your poise, and you may save a friendship. On the other hand, if the criticism is just, thank them for it and ask for their advice."

Dad used this procedure with great effect.

He was traveling by train in the chair car from Binghamton, New York, to Philadelphia, Pennsylvania, seated next to a prominent Philadelphia lawyer. The lawyer engaged my father in conversation. During the conversation, the lawyer remarked on the headlines of the paper. My father said, "It appears to me that this development could be a fulfillment of Bible prophecy."

"I disagree," protested the lawyer with some vigor.

"You can't."

"But I certainly can. I am free, intelligent, and articulate. I certainly can disagree with you." The lawyer was now quite worked up emotionally.

Finally, my father said, "I didn't say what it appears to you; I said what it appears to me."

"Oh," said the lawyer.

Not satisfied to let my father win that round, as it were, the lawyer said, "Now tell me, Reverend, if Adam had never sinned, would the death of Jesus Christ on the cross have been necessary?"

Though the question sounded innocent enough, he was again indulging in a brand of criticism that endeavored to "put down" my father.

Dad, who had been trained in law though he did not reveal that to his traveling companion, said, "I thought you were a lawyer."

"I am," said the lawyer with some force.

"Well," said my father, "Are you practicing currently?"

"I am."

"Where?"

"In Philadelphia. In fact, I practice before the State Supreme Court."

My father said, "And in that court is it permitted to ask hypothetical questions?"

"Oh," said the lawyer, realizing that Dad had answered his challenging question without answering it.

It is true that my father was winding the lawyer up a little. He did not mean to. He innocently enough made an observation as part of what appeared to be a casual and entertaining conversation. Had my father not handled the situation the way he did, the relationship could have turned sour.

When people badmouth you

In 1965, a prominent evangelist made some vicious accusations about me. He did not know me that well. He had no basis, in fact, for the accusations. I was just about to pick up the phone and call him (since the Bible says that we must not allow things like this to "fester") when I received a call from Wichita, Kansas, where I had held a citywide crusade in the Forum in 1960.

The chairman of the committee had been instructed to invite me to return for a citywide crusade. I told him that I was honored by the invitation to return to one of America's great cities, but that I must decline since my schedule was full for the next three years.

He then asked me if I had a recommendation. I said, "Yes," and I recommended this man who was criticizing me all over the nation.

In about a week, I received a letter from the Wichita committee, in which they asked, "Are you aware of what this fellow is saying about you? Are you sure we ought to invite him for a meeting?"

I phoned the chairman and said (with my tongue in my cheek), "Though he, unlike you and I, does not understand what a perfectly wonderful person I am, he is a capable man, a great preacher, a good evangelist, and the Lord will bless the city through his ministry."

On my recommendation, they invited him to come. He came. Though I never did get to see him and though I never heard from him, I learned that thousands of people in the Wichita area were positively influenced by his outstanding ministry.

You find out what people really think when they're mad at you

Anyone in leadership knows that criticism goes with the job. You constantly have to make decisions, and with every option you choose, there will be somebody waiting to tell you what a big mistake you've made.

Clergy probably come in for more criticism than any other profession. If the minister wears a black suit, the critics say, "Who does he think he is—Digger O'Dell?" If he wears a sport coat, the critics question, "What is he trying to do, imitate a movie star?"

If he has five children, critics say, "He can't afford such a family. Why doesn't he use better sense?" If he has only one child, they quip, "Doesn't he know the Bible says that we are to be 'fruitful and multiply'?"

If he visits the poor, they say he is showing off. If he visits the rich, they say he is playing politics.

If he drives a Mercedes Benz, they say he ought to drive a car priced within his means. If he drives a Toyota Corolla, they say, "What's he trying to do, embarrass us by letting people think we don't pay him enough?"

If he preaches 40 minutes, they say he is longwinded. If he preaches 20 minutes they ask, "What's the matter, didn't he study last week?"

If he leaves town for important speaking engagements, they complain, "He ought to stay home and take care of the flock." If he stays home and never goes away, they howl, "What's the matter, doesn't anyone else want him either?"

My father gave me some good advice when I entered the ministry. He said, "John, listen to what people say when they are mad. That's what they really mean."

A man flies off the handle. He says some nasty things. After he cools down he comes back and says, "I really didn't mean that." Of course he meant it! If he had not thought it, he would not have said it, for God's Word makes it clear that "out of the abundance of the heart the mouth speaketh" (Matthew 12:34b). He didn't draw those words and thoughts out of thin air. They were in his heart beforehand.

While I am no disciple of Freud, I do believe in the so-called Freudian slips. When a person writes me a letter in longhand and crosses out one word and writes down another, I have been known to spend 15 or 20 minutes holding that letter up to the light, trying to decipher the word crossed out. In all probability that was what he really meant.

There is another lesson here, of course. Angry criticism can arouse an angry response in you. When you answer criticism volcanically, however, you lose possession of many of your faculties. Your thoughts become inaccurate, your decisions unwise, and your words regrettable.

How to cope at the critical moment

Let me tell you a little habit I have formed that has served me well.

As I have admitted, by nature I am very explosive. After all, I am half-Syrian, and people from that part of the world are not famous for being phlegmatic. When God called me into the ministry, He impressed upon me the fact that by His grace my spirit must be completely dominated by Him if I were to be an effective ambassador of the Court of Heaven.

I memorized and meditated upon 2 Timothy 2:24,25: "The servant of the Lord must not strive; but be gentle unto all men, apt to teach, patient. In meekness instructing those that oppose themselves; if God peradventure will give them repentance to the acknowledging of the truth."

Now here is the procedure I have followed when the provocation of unjust criticism has sorely tempted me to lose my head.

Through sheer conscious effort I try to listen objectively. I look at the person who is venting his anger on me. But I do not see him, for I am imagining myself as a huge elephant walking down the street. Over by the curb (and, I am sometimes inclined to think, in the gutter) a little ant is spitting at the elephant. Ludicrous? Precisely. It helps my sense of humor. Now then, does the elephant feel threatened by the ant? Of course not. Does the elephant stop and get involved in an argument? Of course not. The elephant just serenely moves on by.

All I can say is that this certainly works for me and I have no copyright on it. It keeps me in complete possession of my faculties so that I can think clearly and quickly, talk judiciously, and act wisely.

An American statesman was once quoted as saying, "Never lose your temper, unless you do it on purpose." That's a statement worth thinking about.

Let's go back to Abraham Lincoln for just a moment. While he was an occupant of the White House, some loquacious "smut sprayers" and "character assassinators" spread the rumor that he was living with a black woman. What did the President do? Nothing. This man of poise had learned that in a fight with a skunk you might win the fight, but you will smell awful afterwards!

A vital relationship with God through Christ will result naturally in self-control. When you possess self-control, you will refuse to respond to criticism with smug complacence, worldly courtesy, patronizing condescension, or vindictive retaliation. You will respond with love that is not compatible with worry-producing fear:

> *There is no fear in love; but perfect love casteth out fear: because fear hath torment. He that feareth is not made perfect in love.*
>
> —1 JOHN 4:18

12

POISE THROUGH ENTHUSIASM

It was once my privilege to have an interview with Ray Jenkins, the brilliant lawyer from Knoxville, Tennessee, who presided over the Army-McCarthy hearings in Washington, D.C. during the 1950s. In the course of a conversation I asked him his formula for success in speaking. He mentioned several things, but one thing remains paramount in my mind. He said, "Don't ever speak on a subject about which you are not totally enthused."

Emotion motivates

Enthusiasm is an indispensable ingredient of poise. Some pseudo-intellectuals may take exception to enthusiasm and insist that we do everything on the basis of cool reason alone. I reply simply that most of what we do is done on the basis of emotional rather than intellectual impulse. I do not love my wife because of an intellectual theory about her. Rather, I love her because of an emotional impulse.

Similarly, you did not buy that insurance policy because of some fine calculation of the odds that you might die in the next five years. No doubt calculation comes into it, but the main inducement was strictly emotional. You saw your family destitute and in want because of inadequate material resources. It was this emotional reaction that led you to buy the insurance policy.

Or go to a football game. There you can tell no difference in behavior between the spectator with a third-grade education and the one with several doctoral degrees. They both respond emotionally, with enthusiasm, when their team scores.

One of my hobbies is reading books on salesmanship. I have a collection of more than 50. Without exception, each book on salesmanship underscores enthusiasm as an essential quality for success.

The leaders of this world always have been men and women of enthusiasm. Adolph Hitler knew the power of enthusiasm. His formula for speaking was, "Say it simply. Say it often. Make it burn." Thanks in part to this insight, the Austrian decorator became a world figure who could not be ignored.

Paul the apostle was a man of enthusiasm, as his own autobiographical remarks in Galatians 1:14 and Acts 22:3 attest. He was so enthusiastic about the gospel that some of the people in Corinth accused him of madness (see 2 Corinthians 5:13).

Faith and enthusiasm ought to mix

The person who never wonders at anything never does anything wonderful.

That helps to explain why the work of the Lord suffers so across the land. Thousands of people who profess a relationship with God through Jesus Christ have apparently failed to grasp what Christ has done for them and what their privileges are in Him.

That's why they come to church on Sunday morning with a face long enough to eat ice cream out of a pipe. You could ruin the greatest football team in the nation just by filling the grandstands for four consecutive games with the average Sunday morning congregation. No wonder other belief systems—New Age, Islam—continue to spread while the religion of Jesus Christ fails to keep pace with the population increase of the world.

It's not hard to find people with a passion for movies, opera, fashion, surfboarding, or computer games. But sometimes you'd be hard put to find the same kind of emotional response to the gospel of Christ. Next Sunday when you go to church, watch the average person as he comes in. He shuffles along, dragging his lower lip behind him. Then he slides into the pew and hangs his lower lip over the pew in front of him. He looks as happy as the skull and crossbones on an iodine bottle. No wonder he has no peace of mind.

Remember: You cannot act one way and feel another way. When you act sour, you become sour. Some people who profess "religion" have talked about it for so long in negative terms that those whom they influence have come to see it as blight.

I heard about a man who walked into a hotel lobby and stood beside another man at the room clerk's counter. The fellow eyed his neighbor for a moment, and then could not restrain himself from asking, "Are you a preacher?" "No," the other replied. "I've just been sick!"

And I can well understand the little girl who came home from Sunday school and, going up to Betsy, the mule, lovingly stroked her long head and said, "Bless you, Betsy, you must be a wonderful Christian. You look just like Grandma."

Not only is a lack of enthusiasm ruinous to the work of the Lord, it is also ruinous to happiness in the home, success in business, the making and keeping of friends, and achievement in any field.

Enthusiasm creates passion

There is no such thing as a well-adjusted personality apart from enthusiasm. There is no such thing as a satisfactory social relationship apart from enthusiasm. You reap what you sow. If you sow the wind you will reap the whirlwind. If you sow a deadpan expression, that is exactly what others will give back to you. For what you give out you receive back in kind, only to a greater degree. That's a fact borne out by long years of observation.

As the Bible wisely says: "Whatsoever thy hand findeth to do, do it with thy might; for there is no work, nor device, nor knowledge, nor wisdom, in the grave, whither thou goest" (Ecclesiastes 9:10).

Enthusiasm is like steam. It pressurizes, empowers, impels action. Many people never become enthusiastic over anything, therefore they never achieve anything. Their lives become idle and negative and worrisome.

You know people, and so do I, who constantly complain that they don't get enough sleep. They lament that they wake up every morning feeling as tired as when they went to bed. But what happens when they plan something they really want to do—a holiday, or a fishing trip? They are awake before the alarm sounds at four o'clock in the morning—and feeling great! The explanation? Enthusiasm! All things being equal, the person who is enthusiastic turns out twice as much work as the person who is listless.

Enthusiasm is the key to career success

No great work has ever been done without enthusiasm. Look around you at the great leaders of industry, the great media figures, the great sports personalities. Without exception, they are driven by enthusiasm. They focus on the one thing that motivates them, and the power of that motivation emerges in high performance.

To be sure, some people seem to be born with a greater capacity for enthusiasm than others. But that doesn't mean you can't cultivate it. You can develop enthusiasm. Concentrate your mind on a worthwhile goal until the attainment of that goal becomes your obsession.

The salesmen who succeed vibrate with enthusiasm. Their enthusiastic belief in the product they sell turbocharges their sales. Musicians who succeed beam with enthusiasm. Who can watch a great conductor at the head of one of the world's great orchestras, and not feel the enthusiasm that drives that person to prominence? I submit to you that achievement is impossible without enthusiasm.

If you go about your daily responsibilities in a listless and lackadaisical spirit, devoid of enthusiasm, I can tell you right here and now that you are doomed to mediocrity at best and failure at worst. Not only that, but your failure will create anxiety and worry, and that anxiety and worry will loop back to compound the failure and make it a permanent feature of your life. You will dig yourself into a hole.

You can be enthusiastic anywhere and in any circumstance

Remember that you cannot focus your attention upon two thoughts at the same time. When you are enthused, you focus your attention on positive thoughts that crowd out fears and worries. It doesn't matter how many things seem to be going wrong in your life.

See, for instance, how much the apostle Paul could have complained about:

*Of the Jews five times received I forty stripes save one.
Thrice was I beaten with rods, once was I stoned,
thrice I suffered shipwreck, a night and a day I have
been in the deep; in journeyings often, in perils of
waters, in perils of robbers, in perils by mine own
countrymen, in perils by the heathen, in perils in the
city, in perils in the wilderness, in perils in the sea, in
perils among false brethren; in weariness and painful-
ness, in watchings often, in hunger and thirst, in fast-
ings often, in cold and nakedness. Beside those things
that are without, that which cometh upon me daily,
the care of all the churches.*

—2 CORINTHIANS 11:24-28

Did Paul worry? Did he fret? No! A godly enthusiasm
delivered him from self-pity and worry. Ponder the poise
he achieved through cultivating enthusiasm:

*We are troubled on every side, yet not distressed; we
are perplexed, but not in despair; persecuted, but not
forsaken; cast down, but not destroyed. . . . for which
cause we faint not; but though our outward man
perish, yet the inward man is renewed day by day. For
our light affliction, which is but for a moment, worketh for us a far more exceeding and eternal weight of
glory.*

—2 CORINTHIANS 4:8,9,16,17

13

POISE THROUGH
RELAXATION

In the late 1970s, my young colleague Dr. Michael Youssef and I were waiting for the delayed takeoff of a Pan American flight from Miami to Rio de Janeiro. Our destination was Sao Paulo, where I was to lead a seminar the following day. Finally, at 11 o'clock at night, the plane started rumbling down the runway. I turned to Michael and said, "I'm going to turn on my light and do some reading."

In what seemed just moments later, I was aware that the plane was still rumbling down the runway. I turned to Michael and said, "When in the world are we going to take off?"

He replied, "This is Caracas, Venezuela. You have been sleeping so hard since we left Miami that we couldn't even shake you awake for the meal."

We stayed on the ground in Caracas for an hour. I then slept the four hours from Caracas to Rio de Janeiro. We made a quick transfer flight to Sao Paulo. I cleaned up, shaved, combed my hair. When we disembarked in Sao Paulo, I was ready for a full day's work.

Michael said, "Chief, I am willing to go anywhere with you, but the next time I'm going to leave two days early."

I said to him what I've said to people all over the world: "One of the best investments of discipline and effort you can make is in learning how to relax. Get proper rest, whether it be eight hours end to end, or six hours with snoozes throughout the day. Do whatever is the best for you, but make sure you do it." This leader, with a demanding global ministry, has learned the secret. He has more stamina at 52 than he did at 27.

Put relaxation in your diary

Poise and relaxation go together like bread and butter or ham and eggs. You cannot maintain poise while you are tense. But by the same token, you cannot relax and worry at the same time.

Learn how to work under pressure without working under tension. This is possible if you have periodic breaks in your activities. Breaks don't have to mean inactivity. The break may simply be a *change* in activity.

That's the way your heart works—and boy, does your heart have to stay on the job! Did you know your heart pumps enough blood through your body every 24 hours to fill a railway tanker? Every day it exerts as much effort as it would take to shovel 20 tons of gravel onto a platform as high as your waist.

A lot of people say, "I can't relax; I've got too much to do." If you think to excuse your tension in this way, forget it! No one has had the responsibilities that fell upon our blessed Lord. If anyone had cause for tension, He had. Yet He always remained relaxed. Even when they sought to kill Him (Nazareth, Luke 4), He moved quietly and unhurriedly out of their midst. Can you picture our Lord in a frenzied hurry?

Sure, He took His work seriously: "I must work the works of him that sent me, while it is day: the night cometh, when no man can work" (John 9:4). But He kept His pace.

On occasions when others tried to pressure Him, He said, in substance, "My opportunity is not yet come. The time is not fulfilled." Jesus Christ is our Exemplar in poise through relaxation. Hear Him as He says, "Come ye yourselves apart into a desert place, and rest a while" (Mark 6:31).

The lesson is clear: come apart, or fall apart! It's too easy to be in a rush, driven by a relentless work schedule, and allow insufficient food, insufficient exercise, and insufficient sleep to erode your effectiveness. It's always an easy excuse to say you're busy. But being busy can boil down to a state of perpetual nervous tension—a biochemical high you can't come down from until circumstances get the better of you.

As the Bible reminds us:

> *Don't worry over anything whatever; tell God every detail of your needs in earnest and thankful prayer, and the peace of God, which transcends human understanding, will keep constant guard over your hearts and minds as they rest in Christ Jesus.*

> —PHILIPPIANS 4:6

Finding your rhythm can double your effectiveness

There is a rhythm, a cadence, in all of nature.

Plants reproduce themselves in their seasons and human beings in their generation. There is a rhythm, a cadence, in all the actions of nature: in our breathing, in the ebbing and flowing of the tide, in the rising and setting of the sun. One of the earmarks of the amateur musician is that he or she does not give proper attention to the rests.

Apparently Thomas Edison got by on four hours of sleep a day. However, he had the ability to "snooze" at almost any hour of the day or night. He was relaxed at all times. One of the most prominent of our contemporary psychologists has suggested that we need rest for the body and sleep for the mind. He goes on further to say that the man who stays free of psychic tensions gets by on less sleep than the man who gets tied up in knots.

The last year that Dr. Robert G. Lee served as president of the Southern Baptist Convention (the world's largest Protestant denomination) he was in his late sixties. During that year he traveled over 150,000 miles, built an auditorium that cost more than $17 million in year 2000 dollars. He also received over 1,200 new members into the 9000-member Bellevue Baptist Church in Memphis, Tennessee, of which he was pastor.

One of his members, a prominent Memphis surgeon, Dr. J. Murray Davis, told me that the secret of Dr. Lee's output was his capacity to relax. Dr. Davis said, "It is incredible how this man maintains such a pace despite his years." Then the surgeon recounted this incident in the life of Dr. Lee:

> *One Sunday morning I went to make my hospital visits at six o'clock. Dr. Lee was also at the hospital visiting. He then taught our Sunday school class that morning and followed that by the delivery of one of his matchless sermons at the 11 o'clock hour. Immediately after the morning service he flew by chartered plane to Longview, Texas, where he delivered a baccalaureate address Sunday afternoon. He flew back to Memphis in time to speak at a special assembly of the Baptist Training Union in our church. Following that he delivered the evening message at the 7:30 evangelistic hour. After the benediction of the evening service he rushed to the airport where he boarded a plane for California. He flew all night and spoke Monday night to a large convocation in California.*

What a pace! And remember, he was at an age when many folks have already retired. For more than a quarter of a century Dr. Lee averaged 11 visits a day. He preached in his own church a minimum of three times a week and he taught a Sunday school class 44 Sundays out of every year. After he was 40 years of age, he built a church from a membership of 1,300 to a membership of more than 9,000—while all the time traveling and preaching outside his own city and preaching nearly as often as an evangelist.

The secret? He knew how to relax! He knew how to pace himself! He worked under pressure without working under tension.

Relaxation helps older people hyperperform

Learn the rhythm of successful living. When you work, work. When you rest, rest.

When my father was 62 years of age he pastored a vigorous church in New York State. He slept only a few hours a night. He walked two miles a day. He was one of the best paddleball players in Binghamton, New York, and all his opponents were under 35. On his sixtieth birthday he played two sets of tennis. How did he do it? He knew how to relax.

On several occasions, when I visited him, he would sit in his high-back rocking chair. Right in the middle of our conversation he would say, "You must excuse me, son. I am going to take a few minutes' snooze." He'd lay his head back and sleep for perhaps seven minutes, then open his eyes again, fresh and alert, and say, "All right, now. Where were we?"

Most great achievers maintain the practice of having a nap sometime during the day. It has been proven that a person will fare better with six hours of sleep at night and an hour of sleep every afternoon than with eight hours of sleep at night with no break in the day.

As a young man I realized that if I were to be productive, I would have to master the ability to relax and to sleep. I worked at it assiduously. In the late 1960s, I boarded a flight from Seattle to Tokyo. Then-head of World Vision, Dr. Ted Engstrom, was on the same flight. He said, "John, people tell me that you can sleep like a baby on these flights, and you don't even take a sleeping pill. I don't believe it."

I grinned and said, "Well, Ted, I'm grateful to God. It's true."

Our flight lifted off. We had a meal, after which I read a paper and thumbed through a magazine. About an hour and a half out of Seattle, I stretched across the three seats and laid my head on three pillows just under the window. I slept soundly until 30 minutes out of Tokyo. Ted couldn't believe it.

There's no way that I could have maintained my schedule over the past 40 years had I not learned the secret of relaxation. In that time, I have made more than 85 trips around the world plus more than 167 intercontinental trips; written 15 books and hundreds of inches of copy for brochures, appeal letters, and magazine articles; averaged a speech nearly once a day; administrated an organization with offices on every inhabited continent; and maintained my own personal study habits and responsibilities.

Were it not for my ability to relax, I would be a physical and emotional basket case by this time. At an age that some consider well past retirement, I thank God I'm still able to function with a great deal of energy and zest. The key? The ability to relax.

Relaxation is a vital component of poise. The soil of tension and frenzy will produce long green shoots of worry. Therefore, ask God to help you find poise through relaxation.

14

POISE THROUGH
SCHEDULING

During the 1970s, Korean Presbyterians invited me to be the evangelist for the Seventh Decade Spiritual Revolution Crusade.

The chairman of that event was Dr. Kyung Chik Han, pastor of the world's largest Presbyterian church—the Young Nak (meaning "eternal joy") Church in Seoul. The crusade lasted for three weeks, with one week being spent in each of three cities—Pusan, Taegu, and Seoul.

For 21 days I was honored to be in the company of this distinguished world leader. Twice dispossessed of all—literally all—his earthly goods, Dr. Han had known the scourge of Japan's cruel occupation in the 1940s and North Korea's atheistic terrorism in the 1950s.

What I learned from Dr. Han

In 1956, with 27 North Korean refugees, Dr. Han founded the Young Nak Church. Just after the outer structure of the new sanctuary was completed, the North Koreans stormed across the 38th parallel and into Seoul, driving freedom-loving Koreans southward and nearly into the sea. The new sanctuary was used by the North Koreans as an ammunition depot.

Dr. Han and his people established three other Young Nak churches during their southern exile. Back in Seoul in 1963, the work continued, and the statistics are impressive. The membership climbed to more than 16,000 by 1972. More than 100 daughter churches were established. In addition, Dr. Han and his colleagues founded schools, orphanages, senior citizens' quarters, summer camps, spiritual retreat grounds and facilities, and special ministries among the military groups. Such was the quality of Dr. Han's leadership.

Yet, the dear man never appeared harried or hurried. I watched for three weeks for any sign of pique or impatience. I never saw it.

Dr. Han met with his people every morning for the five o'clock to six o'clock dawn prayer meeting. What a way to start every day!

His life was a model of quiet achievement for Christ. He was the master teacher of the stewardship of time. I have heard him lecture on the subject. Better, I have watched him put his teaching into practice. He so scheduled his time—so planned his work and worked his plan—that he could discharge Herculean responsibilities.

He knew God had given him adequate time to achieve all that lay within the divine will for his work in Korea. In complete dependence upon the Holy Spirit of God, he moved peacefully and productively. Consistently relaxed and gracious, he infused this mood on all those who worked with him.

Dr. Han's life was a symphony of poise. The atmosphere of his home made it into a vestibule of heaven. Fellowship with this man of God bestowed its own special benediction.

Hurry doesn't pay

Life in the twenty-first century grows ever more frenetic. Fast travel, mobile phones, and e-mail have made us far more accessible than we used to be. We move faster. We do more. And there is more to do. It is the easiest thing in the world to lose your poise under the pressure of work.

By scheduling your activities you will make great strides toward victory in this area.

Scheduling defeats frenzy and hurry. It does this by bringing regularity into lifestyle and by imposing order on what otherwise might be a chaotic, moment-to-moment existence. Hurry is symptomatic of a weakly organized mind. Without scheduling and organization you will move fast and make mistakes, and that will lead to discouragement and tension.

Let me suggest that you read the autobiography of Benjamin Franklin. He tells of his effort to master the 13 virtues. He was past 80 years of age when he wrote the autobiography, and at this milestone he was forced to admit that order was the one virtue he had never been able to conquer. It is probably one of the most difficult habits to perfect.

Yet order is so important.

There is a story told of a state psychiatric hospital in Illinois. One day one of the inmates ran out of the gate and down the road as fast as he could run. The orderlies chased him, caught him, and brought him back. The next day another inmate did exactly the same thing with the same result. That happened ten successive days with ten different inmates. Now, if the ten inmates had fled at the same time, and if each had run in a different direction, probably nine of them would have escaped. However, they were not *organized*. Which is probably why they were in the institution in the first place.

Plan your work and work your plan

Ask God for the wisdom to help you plan your work, then ask Him for the grace to let you work your plan. "The Lord is near," so call upon Him for the needed wisdom and grace.

God led Nehemiah to plan for the rebuilding of the Jerusalem walls. He led Nehemiah in the seemingly impossible feat of organizing labor and resources to achieve the task in the teeth of unspeakable opposition. In the same way, the Lord will enable you, if you will but call upon Him, to so plan your work and work your plan that you will fulfill the divine injunction to be "always abounding in the work of the Lord" (1 Corinthians 15:58).

Fatigue is caused mostly by boredom. When you have no order—when you have failed to schedule your activities—you lack the awareness of accomplishment. Conversely, when you have wisely scheduled your activities under the leadership of the Holy Spirit, and when you are performing your responsibilities on schedule, you get a natural lift. There is nothing more invigorating than the awareness of tasks efficiently completed, and there is nothing more dispiriting than the knowledge of unfulfilled responsibilities.

List your tasks at the start of the day. As you complete them, check them off. When you reach the end of your workday, contemplate the satisfaction of five, ten, fifteen, or twenty tasks successfully accomplished.

Paul enjoins us to be "redeeming the time, because the days are evil" (Ephesians 5:16). By God's grace and in His strength, we will fulfill our responsibility to redeem the time. In doing that we will conquer worry through poise by scheduling.

The Lord gives us the ability and the time to do *everything* He expects us to do. We have an obligation—and a privilege—to utilize these God-given resources so that His will for us may be fulfilled. And in turn that fulfillment honors Him and dispels anxiety. God help us to live in such a way—as our Lord while yet on earth was able to do—so that we can say, "I have finished the work which thou gavest me to do" (John 17:4b).

15

POISE THROUGH VARIETY

Not long ago a filmmaker produced a full-length movie in which the screen remained a consistent shade of blue from beginning to end. It was called—you guessed it—*Blue*. No doubt the director in question had good reasons for making such a film, but it never went on general release for one very simple reason: sitting in a movie theatre looking at a blue screen is just not very exciting. It's also painful on the eyes.

Human beings were made for variety. We thrive on it. And as in filmmaking, so in conversation. People whose talk is in only one color do not command respect from others or attract their interest. The proverb remains true: "Variety is the spice of life."

Paul had interests outside the gospel

Does that seem like an almost blasphemous statement? How could Paul, the great apostle, who was so consumed with his evangelistic mission, possibly have taken an interest in anything else?

Yet he clearly did. The apostle Paul was not only a preacher; he was also a logician. Apparently he was interested in athletics, because he alluded to athletics many times in his epistles. Furthermore, his reference to Greek poets in Acts 17 indicates he was conversant with poetry. Certainly no one could deny that he was also a master at understanding human nature. And these interests did not detract from his mission. Rather, they made him more able to communicate what really mattered: the good news of salvation in Christ.

Similarly, David the king was a sportsman, a poet, a musician, a militarist, and a philosopher. And who could adequately evaluate the multiplicity of interests maintained by his son Solomon?

> *And he spake three thousand proverbs: and his songs were a thousand and five. And he spake of trees, from the cedar tree that is in Lebanon even unto the hyssop that springeth out of the wall: he spake also of beasts, and of fowl, and of creeping things, and of fishes.*
>
> —1 KINGS 4:32,33

You will see from this that Solomon was a sage, a musician, a poet, a horticulturist, an expert in animal husbandry, an ornithologist, an entomologist, and a piscatologist. Presumably, had he not been good company, the Queen of Sheba would not have come all that way to meet him.

Or take the example of our own Lord. Study His parables and you will conclude that He knew not only what went on in the depths of the human heart, but what kinds of lives the people around him lived. Because he was so well grounded in these things, Jesus could talk easily with men and women of every background, race, and social rank. All listened to Him with absorption. He could appeal to the educated Nicodemus just as He could to the fishermen and the woman of ill repute from Samaria.

A diversity of interests keeps a balance essential to poise. It gives a sense of perspective. It assists in communication. And it brings a wealth of experience, which is one of the gifts God has given humankind.

The Bible shows us that such interests should be actively cultivated.

When Paul the apostle was forced out of Berea by persecution, he did not go to Athens and brood. He kept busy. In Athens he went down to the marketplace and listened to the dialogues of the philosophers. He studied the habit patterns of the Athenians. There he discovered what interested and motivated them.

This study quickly bore fruit. It wasn't long before they insisted he go to Areopagus, to the top of Mars Hill, where only the great orators and the celebrities were permitted to speak. There he delivered the most masterful sermon ever preached by any man—our Lord excepted, of course. An interest in life's variety resourced his communication.

No one can honor God in a maximum way whose only interests lie within the boundaries of a narrow and specialized field. Without a variety of interests, you will not keep anyone's attention for long.

Variety keeps you balanced—even in the pulpit

I know from my own experience that the pressures on clergy are phenomenal. They are on call 24 hours a day, 7 days a week. They never have the satisfaction of knowing that everything is done. There is always another person to visit, another letter to write, another message to prepare. Besides this, they are the CEOs of their organizations, handling any number of sensitive interpersonal issues, and maintaining not only a paid staff but a large body of volunteer leaders. No wonder an article recently published in the American press was titled "Why Ministers Are Cracking Up."

Time and again, I have seen that great ministers in tough pastorates not only survive but empower their ministries by keeping other interests alive.

The brilliant pulpit orator from Louisiana, Dr. James W. Middleton, went through enough tribulations to shatter the nerves of five rugged men. In the midst of his metropolitan ministry a serious throat condition requiring surgery put him out of his pulpit for nearly a year. The experience put his entire ministry in jeopardy. Yet he returned to scale new heights in the proclamation of God's Word—a feat explained in no small measure by the broad base of his interests, which included horticulture, hunting, and fishing.

Dr. Roy O. McClain, former pastor of the First Baptist Church of Atlanta, Georgia, and selected in 1957 by *Time* magazine as one of the ten most outstanding American clergymen of that year, seemed to spend every spare hour honing his powers as a speaker and communicator. Yet he had several hobbies, among which were the raising of Shetland ponies, painting, the playing of the organ, and woodworking. He found these hobbies essential. They served as a balance wheel, giving him unruffled poise as he led the largest congregation in Georgia.

It's never too late to start

For years I looked with envy on people who did downhill skiing.

I felt I could not afford the cost, and I knew, without a shadow of a doubt, I could not afford the time. However, I set my goal to take up skiing at 63. On my sixty-third birthday I drove to Hopfgarten, Austria, and for the next two-and-a-half weeks, I enjoyed the professional excellence of Austria's proverbial ski geniuses.

In seven days, I was coming down the steepest slope of Hopfgarten Mountain. In nine days I was coming down without falling over. Before I left, my Austrian friends gave me a videotape made by Austria's Department of Ski Instruction so that during the summer months I could rehearse the various moves by watching the video.

This was the first time I had engaged in an athletic sideline to which I devoted any serious energy, enthusiasm, and resources. I tell you frankly that it proved as effective in undergirding my inner poise and serenity as anything I have ever done. My friend and ski companion, Hank Bronson, a Chicago businessman, served as an ideal example for me. He knows how to relax while leading a major business.

For one thing, you cannot come down a steep ski slope and think about anything else except skiing. It's a marvelous way to force yourself into brushing aside the multitude of energy-sapping little problems that confront you when you reach the office or pick up the morning post.

Now, I'm not suggesting that you take up the same pursuit. I am suggesting that you find some equivalent activity to which you can give wholehearted enthusiasm—a hobby that helps you to relax and that reinforces inner poise. It may be cooking. Or theatre. Or plunging down flooded ravines in a rubber raft. It doesn't have to be complex or expensive. What matters is that you do it.

Work and play can be the same thing

For some people, variety seems to mean coming home from work and plopping into a chair in front of the television. In truth, they are not getting much out of the riches life can offer them. Avoid like the plague passive variety. In Mark 6:31, when Jesus said to the apostles, "Come ye yourselves apart. . . and rest awhile," they did not lie down under an olive tree and sleep. Rather, they went out to eat, and then they engaged in a different form of activity. Variety means finding other outlets for expression, not switching yourself off. Jesus was always busy about His Father's business; He just varied the mode of his activity.

The world-famed industrialist R. G. LeTourneau once had an important appointment in his plant at Toccoa, Georgia. While in flight to Georgia, the pilot of his plane discovered that the landing gear was stuck. The pilot radioed ahead to the airport in Anderson, South Carolina, and told them the problem. Ambulances and a rescue squad rushed to the airport. The news media arrived to cover the event. The plane made a good crash landing. But when LeTourneau got out of the plane his first words had nothing to do with the plane. He said, in substance, "Where's the car? I am already late for my appointment in Toccoa. Can you get me a car immediately?"

There is poise. I asked him one time when he took his vacation. He said, "I never take a vacation. My work is my play and you never need a vacation from play." There was a man who, through Christ and wise self-discipline, learned the poise that conquers worry.

16

POISE THROUGH
SEIZING THE DAY

Yesterday is a cashed check and cannot be negotiated. Tomorrow is a promissory note and cannot be utilized today. Today is cash in hand. Spend it wisely.

The songwriter D. W. Whittle understood this truth when he wrote:

> *Moment by moment I'm kept in His love,*
> *Moment by moment I've life from above.*
> *Looking to Jesus till glory doth shine;*
> *Moment by moment, O, Lord, I am thine.*

The trouble with many people is that instead of looking to Jesus they are looking to tomorrow, waiting for circumstances to turn and favor them. What a tragic waste of opportunity. The psalmist tells us, "This is the day which the LORD hath made; we will rejoice and be glad in it" (Psalm 118:24). Lowell Thomas had these words framed and hung on the walls of his broadcasting studio at his farm so that he could see them often.

If the conviction of your heart is summed up in this verse, it is impossible for you to worry.

There is no point in living in the past. Paul was in the habit of "forgetting those things which are behind" (Philippians 3:13). All your opportunities and responsibilities lie right here in the present. So give every moment your all. Give your entire attention to the work at hand, the person with whom you are talking or dealing. The Lord grants us time only here and now. You can use each moment only once.

God will give you what you need today

Many people say, "If only this or that would change, then I could reach my goals." Nonsense! God gives you today exactly what you need today.

The Bible illustrates this principle perfectly in the story of the manna falling on the children of Israel in Exodus 16. Read the passage:

> *This is the thing which the LORD hath commanded, Gather of it every man according to his eating, an omer for every man, according to the number of your persons. . . . And the children of Israel did so, and gathered, some more, some less. And when they did mete it with an omer, he that gathered much had nothing over, and he that gathered little had no lack; they gathered every man according to his eating. And Moses said, Let no man leave of it till the morning. Notwithstanding they hearkened not unto Moses; but some of them left of it until the morning, and it bred worms, and stank. . . .*
>
> —EXODUS 16:16-20

The Israelites were in need of food. They needed it today, tomorrow, and the day after that. But the Lord provided for them a *daily supply.* He did not send down manna in seven-day sacks. If they gathered more than they needed for the day, all the excess rotted. The truth is simply this: God's sustenance comes to you now, right at this moment. You cannot have this day again, and so you must make the best job of it you can. Whatever God wants you to do today, He has given you the resources to do.

Jesus lived and worked in the "now"

Here again our Lord is *the* example. He came to die. Through His death He set up a kingdom—a kingdom not of this world, but a spiritual kingdom. Said Jesus, "To this end was I born, and for this cause came I into the world" (John 18:37).

The shadow of persecution and death constantly lay across Jesus' path. Nevertheless, He lived one day at a time and did not permit the grief, torture, and pain that faced Him to rob Him of perfect composure for today. Little children reveled in His company. Men who conversed with Him were aware of His total absorption with *their* problems. Over and over again we can hear our Lord saying, "My hour is not yet come." In other words, He lived moment by moment, one day at a time. Observe His matchless poise!

Don't be forever living in the future. It's true that as a Christian, you are to look unceasingly for the blessed hope and glorious appearing of Jesus Christ. But as you do so, don't neglect your present work. Live in such a way that you will never be ashamed to meet Jesus, whenever He appears.

In Acts 1:6 the followers of our Lord asked, "Lord, wilt thou at this time restore again the kingdom to Israel?"

Consider the answer our Lord gave: "It is not for you to know the times or the seasons, which the Father hath put in his own power. But ye shall receive power, after that the Holy Ghost is come upon you . . ." (Acts 1:7,8).

Our Lord replied by showing them that the finest possible preparation they could make for the future was a Spirit-led execution of the present. The proof that the child of God is looking forward to the second coming of Christ is his faithfulness in living *today* for the glory of God.

The Today Principle is widely applied

Montaigne said, "My life has been full of terrible misfortunes, most of which never happened." Many of us might say the same thing. How foolish of us to scuttle our opportunities and waste the privileges of this day which is slipping away with fantastic speed.

John Ruskin had on his desk a simple piece of stone on which was sculptured one word: *TODAY.*

Osler gives good advice when he says, "Banish the future; live only for the hour and its allotted work. . . . Set earnestly at the little task at your elbow . . . our plain duty is 'not to see what lies dimly at a distance, but to do what lies clearly at hand.'"

Yes, seize today! Richard Baxter left to us sage advice when he said, "Spend your time in nothing which you know must be repented of; in nothing on which you might not claim the blessings of God; in nothing which you could not review with a quiet conscience on your dying bed; in nothing which you might not be safely and properly doing if guests surprise you in the act."

Most of your misery is left over from yesterday or borrowed from tomorrow. In the dynamic of the Holy Spirit determine to live today to the glory of God. This is the day that the Lord has made. Paul would remind you to redeem the time, for the days are evil (Ephesians 5:16). God has given you today. He has taken back all your yesterdays. All your tomorrows are still in His keeping.

Living in the "now" for 24 years

I told earlier of how the Lord graciously blessed us with a precious son.

One of the nation's most respected gynecologists and obstetricians brought him into the world. Tragically, this man—overcome by grief—sought to find the answer in a bourbon bottle rather than in the blessed Bible. Due to the doctor's intoxication at the time of delivery, several of the baby's bones were broken. His leg was pulled out at the growing center. Needless abuse—resulting in hemorrhaging of the brain—was inflicted upon the little fellow.

During the first year of his life, eight doctors said he could not possibly survive. Until he was two my wife had to feed him every three hours with a Brecht feeder. It took a half hour to prepare for the feeding and it took another half hour to clean up and put him back to bed. Not once during that time did she get out of the house for any diversion whatsoever. Never did she get more than two hours sleep at one time.

My wife, formerly Christine Barker of Bristol, Virginia, had once been acclaimed by some of the nation's leading musicians as one of the outstanding contemporary female vocalists in America. From the time she was 13 she had been popular as a singer—and constantly in the public eye. Hers was the experience of receiving and rejecting some fancy offers with even fancier incomes to marry an aspiring Baptist pastor with not even a church to his name!

Then, after five years of marriage, tragedy struck. The whole episode was so unnecessary. From a life of public service she was now marooned within the walls of our home. Her beautiful voice no longer enraptured public audiences with the story of Jesus, but was now silenced, or at best, muted to the subdued humming of lullabies.

Had it not been for her spiritual maturity, whereby she laid hold of the resources of God and lived one day at a time, this heartrending experience would long since have caused an emotional breakdown.

John Edmund, Jr., our little son, lived 24 years and died in 1975. We rejoice that he committed his heart and life to Jesus Christ and gave evidence of a genuine concern for the things of the Lord. I attribute his commitment to Jesus Christ and his wonderful disposition to the sparkling radiance of an emotionally mature, Christ-centered mother who has mastered the discipline of living in the "now."

The people who know her concur that, after enduring a grief more intense than most could guess, she still possesses a sparkle that would be the envy of any high school senior, and a radiance and charm for which any debutante would gladly give a fortune.

Don't let others seize the day for you

Seize the day. Live for today. Wring it dry of every opportunity.

You have troubles? So do others. So did Paul, who said, "Most gladly therefore will I rather glory in my infirmities that the power of Christ may rest upon me" (2 Corinthians 12:9b).

You seize the day. Don't let others seize it for you. Peer pressure in the United States robs too many of their individuality. There's no reason for you to engage in socializing just because that's the excessive pastime of your neighbors.

If you want to socialize, if it contributes to your social well-being without imposing counterproductive pressures on you, go to it. However, I am appalled at the excessive and superficial socializing in which otherwise free people allow unproductive activities to enslave them. They permit their minds to be divided between asking, "Is this what I ought to do?" and "What will they think of me if I don't go?" Take control of your own life. Go or don't go. But don't sit on the fence.

Because so many allow themselves to become enslaved to this superficial socializing, they never read a book, never memorize a poem, and never take that course at the university night school they had promised themselves they were going to take. In short, they rob themselves of the really important contributions to their lives and influence.

Seize the day for your children

Unfortunately, our society has developed two extreme types of parents: those who abuse their children, and those who become hostage to them. In either case, I can assure you that the major reason is the divided mind. And in either case, the children suffer.

Let's take the case of the parents who become hostage to their children. They don't want their children to walk from the front door to the pantry. They must drive them there! Jogging for fitness is in. But for children, walking is out. These parents are determined that, whatever the cost, they are to be a spectator at every activity in which the child has a part.

Consequently, we have had a 50-percent increase in obesity among children in the past ten years in the United States. The medical profession unanimously attributes this to too much television and too little exercise.

How many children do you know today who are required to do chores? Even to make up their own beds, help wash the dishes or the car, take care of the lawn, or assist with the housecleaning? I submit to you that in many cases, the parents have split their minds between what they know they ought to do and what their peers are doing down the street.

I was in a vigorous and enjoyable debate with a man from Yorkshire, England. He said, "When I visit your country, I am appalled that so many can't make up their minds."

"What are you talking about?" I protested.

"I'll give you a perfect illustration: Junior asks his mother if he can go to a certain function. His mother then gets on the phone and calls the mothers of all of Junior's neighbors to find out what they are going to do. After having taken a poll of the neighbors, his parents then give Junior the verdict. What a terrible way to rear a lad. They are creating an atmosphere of indecision which is bound to have a negative effect on the boy."

I protested vigorously, but in my mind I knew that—more often than I cared to admit—what he said was true. And why do people act in this manner? The divided mind. It's divided between their responsibility as parents and their fear of falling out of line with their peers. In short, they don't seize the day. They let the day—and their peers—seize them. And that does not make for mental health, emotional stability, or a serene home life.

You develop greater poise when you determine to take time by the forelock and, under the leadership of God, shake it into obedience and make it your servant instead of your master.

People who worry about their health become hostage to the day instead of seizing the day. A friend told me of his mother who worried for 40 years that she would die of cancer. She died at 73–from pneumonia. It's tragic. She wasted 40 years worrying about the wrong thing. Over those 40 years she brought depression instead of delight to the hearts of her closest friends and members of her family. For 40 years she divided her mind and her time between useful pursuits and worrying about cancer. For 40 years her testimony for Christ was dimmed and her witness for Christ was diminished simply because she refused to live one day at a time—and to live that day to the fullest and to the glory of God.

Read it again: "This is the day which the LORD hath made; we will rejoice and be glad in it" (Psalm 118:24). You know it makes sense.

17

POISE THROUGH
SKILL

The preacher M. E. Dodd once said, "Many are twisting a tune out of a hand organ when they ought to be playing a four-manual pipe organ. Many are satisfied to play with mud pies when they ought to be making angel food cakes. Many are crawling when they ought to be running. Many are building shacks when they ought to be building palaces."

It's true. If you want to develop the poise that conquers worry, then do everything you do the best you can and learn to master some skill.

First Corinthians 10:31 says: "Whether therefore ye eat, or drink, or whatsoever ye do, do all to the glory of God." Therefore if we are going to glorify God, we must do our best. There is no room for mediocrity in the life of the child of God. God deserves and demands our best.

Hear ye the Master's call, "Give Me thy best!"
For, be it great or small, that is His test.
Do then the best you can, not for reward,
Not for the praise of men, but for the Lord.

Wait not for men to laud, heed not their slight;
Winning the smile of God brings its delight!
Aiding the good and true ne'er goes unblest,
All that we think or do, be it the best.

Night soon comes on a pace, day hastens by:
Workman and work must face testing on high.
Oh, may we in that day find rest, sweet rest,
Which God has promised those who do their best.

Skill is essential to poise

The speaker who has subjected himself to rigorous discipline until he has perfected the craft of speaking is poised when he speaks. The speaker who has not paid the price of discipline, and who comes to the pulpit or to the lectern half-prepared, lacks poise—and if he has any discernment, he will be tortured to reflect on the mess he has made of it.

The anxiety produced thereby is totally unnecessary and could have been eliminated if he had simply paid the price in developing the needed skill. The same is true for the doctor, the lawyer, the salesman, the artisan, the athlete, the artist, the cook.

For a professing Christian to do less than his best is inexcusable. The Christian has the motive and the resources to achieve true mastery.

It is tragic that there are so few truly great musicians today. So few great orators. So few great financiers. So few great inventors. Thank God, however, that there are still some who are willing to soar to the heights of the eagle, though they know they will fly alone. For the glory of God and for their own peace of mind, they are willing to exert themselves to the full and to climb the ladder of achievement to the topmost rung.

Some time ago I had an interview with one of the greatest speech professors in America. He showed me seven pages of elementary voice exercises, which, to my amazement, he said he had practiced daily for 40 years. This man cannot tolerate mediocrity.

The great pianist Ignacy Paderewski practiced simple finger exercises for hours every day over a period of years. No wonder the musical world 100 years ago was hypnotized by his skill.

Edison experimented hundreds of times before he successfully developed the electric light filament. While he was working on it, a scientist in England went on record as saying that the electric light filament was an impossibility and anyone who said otherwise was a fraud. But Thomas Edison, who loathed mediocrity, kept on giving his best until success crowned his efforts.

Matthew Henry worked hours every day for 40 years in producing his *Commentaries.* They probably appear on the bookshelves of more clergymen than any other Bible commentary set. Why? Because, under God, Matthew Henry gave his best.

Jesus told the parable of the man who started the house but never lived in it. Our Master scorned a task half done.

For years, William Jennings Bryan unrelentingly and laboriously practiced the art of oratory. He never won a speech contest. Nevertheless he kept on. As a comparative unknown he attended the Democratic National Convention held at the Coliseum in Chicago in 1896. It was past midnight. The people were weary. Many of them were leaving. He stepped up to the stand and delivered his famous Cross of Gold oration.

This speech, so masterfully delivered by the man who never won a speech contest, catapulted Bryan into the position of standard-bearer for the Democratic Party. In less than 24 hours he had become a national figure. This mighty man of God had mastered the mechanics of the work for which God had called him, and the record of his life is a glittering trophy and an imposing monument to the glory of God.

Too often we don't try hard enough

Peace of mind is dependent upon the awareness of divine approval. When we fail to give God our best, we fail to bring maximum honor and glory to His name. Consciousness of this failure produces anxiety and inner conflict.

There is no poise like the poise that accompanies mastery of a skill in the power of God.

Whatever your personal view of television, I think you must confess that it presents one of the most stinging rebukes to the apathy of church leadership. Performers will work day and night to attain mastery in the field of show business.

Singer Kate Smith dominated television when I was a younger man. I learned that for every hour she appeared on the screen, she spent 18 hours in preparation. At that time she was broadcasting five hours a week. For five hours of TV entertainment, she willingly worked 90 hours to bring to her viewers the finest programs she was capable of producing. She did not have to do this for monetary reasons, for at the time she was reputedly a millionaire several times over.

On the other hand, consider how shoddily professing Christians will treat the work of the Lord. Here's an example: A soloist gets up to sing. Possibly he has rehearsed that particular number, but more probably he has not. He sticks his nose in the crease of the book and has to read every word. Imagine an opera star bound down to script and music! What conclusion do you come to? Yes, that's right. Evidently, the opera star is more devoted to the mastery of her profession than the average gospel soloist is to the glory of God.

In Philippians 4:13 Paul assures us, "I can do all things through Christ which strengtheneth me." You have the resources necessary to do what God requires of you. And in the fulfillment of His calling, you will have poise that conquers anxiety.

Learn to do at least one thing better than anyone else can do it

It's true of us all that we like to do what we know we can do well. You are less likely to worry if you feel in command of what you are doing. Worry results from a divided mind. When you are doing what you like to do, your mind is occupied with one thing. "This one thing I do," said Paul (Philippians 3:13). Dwight L. Moody added that most people today would have to change this and say, "These 50 things I dabble in."

The high school boy enjoys most the sport he plays best. The teacher feels most confident and comfortable in the subject area she loves and in which she has extensive knowledge. The legendary conductor Leonard Bernstein used to do children's shows on television. For one solid hour he would hold a capacity studio audience of hundreds of children spellbound and charm millions of television viewers. He was totally absorbed. Obviously he enjoyed it. Why? Because he was probably the world's greatest music teacher when it came to explaining music to the masses. He liked to do it because he had mastered the skill of doing it well. At the conclusion of the hour, even the television viewers detected that he was nearly exhausted but supremely happy. He was poised.

There is an important lesson here. At my high school, the principal, who also taught us American history, admonished us over and over again to "learn to do at least one thing better than anyone else can do it."

Have you not had this experience many times? Perhaps it was at a party, or maybe a picnic, that you saw someone who seemed absolutely disengaged from the proceedings, moping around on the sidelines and refusing to participate in the activities.

Then a game or a sport was proposed, and the mention of it brought light into his eyes. He threw himself into that game or sport with everything he had. He was clearly skillful in that activity. And because he was doing something he knew how to do, his body became vibrant. His face shone. His conversation became animated and enthusiastic. In short, he began to show all the evidence of being poised. His skill in the particular activity allowed him to become congenially involved in the group. His mind was no longer divided. His interests were no longer diffused. He had found a place because he could use a skill he had mastered better than anyone else.

The satisfaction of a skill employed

When Bedan Mbugua of Kenya came for a course of advanced Christian leadership training in Singapore, he was a pharmaceutical salesman. Suddenly, however, a fresh idea struck him. He saw the possibility of publishing a magazine that would communicate the gospel of Jesus Christ to people who might never come to church or be interested in religious things.

When he returned to Kenya, he pursued his goal. In less than three years, the magazine he was producing outsold *Time* and *Newsweek* in five African nations, including Nigeria. He later transferred the ownership and production of the magazine to another party, and started yet another publication.

Bedan's story has been one of ever-increasing successes. He loves the work. And he loves it for one reason: because he's good at it. Equally, you could say that he's good at it because he loves it!

I repeat, we like to do what we know how to do well. Bedan Mbugua understands magazine publishing. He not only understands the writing needs, the editorial needs, and the demographics of the areas where he intends to sell, but he also understands the business aspects, marketing techniques, and all of the various elements essential to the production of an influential magazine.

If you want to conquer worry, discipline yourself to the point of mastery in the field to which God has called you. For your own peace of mind, excel in at least one thing. Gather your resources, rally all your faculties, marshal all your energies, focus all your capacities upon mastery in at least one field of endeavor. This is a sure-fire antidote to the divided mind. Stop scattering your efforts. Cease half-hearted attempts to be superb in everything. Ascertain the will of God for your life. Enlist His help and strength, and trust that through Him you can do all things. Strive for mastery, and soon you will experience worry-killing poise through your skill.

18
POISE THROUGH INDUSTRY

The person who said, "I've found a great way to start the day—I go straight back to bed" was very sadly mistaken. Idleness subjects you to destructive thoughts, dangerous impulses, and perilous pressures from without. All these things contribute to anxiety.

Jesus Himself said, "I must work" (John 9:4). He also said, "My Father worketh hitherto, and I work" (John 5:17).

Work is divine in its inception. The old adage "Idleness is the devil's workshop" is true.

Reflect upon the grief that idleness brought David the king. When he should have been in battle, he was at home, taking it easy. While idling about his palace he saw a sight that stirred his sexual passions. Still idle, he reflected and meditated upon that experience until it festered into the open sin of covetousness and then adultery. Those sins in turn led to the murder of Uriah, the husband of Bathsheba. Before long the entire affair was public knowledge. Talk about anxiety! I have no doubt that David at one point would gladly have died rather than lived through the grief and anxiety produced by the harvest of his idleness.

The industry of Paul

Paul the apostle had been pursued by hostility at Berea, and it was necessary for him to flee to Athens—alone! In Athens he could have holed up in some private room and felt sorry for himself. He could have brooded over the mistreatment he had suffered for the work of the Lord. He could have said, "I have been laboring night and day in Thessalonica and preaching faithfully in Berea. Now I will take it easy."

Not Paul. Immediately he began an investigation of conditions in Athens. After acquainting himself with the conditions in this intellectual metropolis, he began to preach in the synagogue to the Jews and among devout people in the marketplace daily. Soon his ministry attracted the interest of the philosophers, the Epicureans and the Stoics. They requested a speech from him in which he would set forth his philosophy. He could have responded, "Oh, no. I was stoned and left for dead at Lystra. I was beaten and jailed in Philippi. I have just now been abused in Berea for this very thing—preaching the gospel of the Son of God, whom I serve."

Paul was not of this stripe, however. Far from feeling sorry for himself, he shared with them the blessed gospel. At their invitation he walked up the stone steps to the top of Areopagus, the ancient heart of Athens from whose crescent of stone seats the judges had 300 years previously condemned Socrates to die. Standing at this place, the ambassador of the Judge of the earth delivered probably the greatest sermon ever to come from the lips of mortal man.

Thorough preparation marked every facet of Paul's ministry. As soon as God had saved him in Damascus, he immediately started preparation in Arabia and then in Jerusalem, developing the skill necessary for the work to which

God had called him (consider this against the backdrop of the preceding chapter). At Athens, Paul was speaking to the intellectual leaders of the world. The laws of this city pronounced death upon anyone introducing a foreign deity. Did that stop Paul? He was a Jewish tentmaker whose "bodily presence is weak, and his speech contemptible" (2 Corinthians 10:10)—but he spoke out in that classic and proud city of the ancient world.

It was in the marketplace at Athens that Socrates, the wisest of men, asked his immortal questions. Over in the nearby olive groves by the brook, Plato founded his academy. To the east was the Lyceum of Aristotle. Near at hand in the Agora were the garden of the Epicureans and the painted porch of the Stoics. Here was the home of ancient Greek drama, where scholars spoke with pride the names of Aeschylus and Sophocles. Here the orators of Greece stood up to speak. Here were historians like Thucydides and Xenophon. In their Athenian temples the national spirit of Athens was deified in the marble images of their heroes and soldiers, in the trophies of her victories, in her multifarious objects of interest. Here Paul introduced a foreign deity, God Almighty.

Here Paul preached:

- The personality of God

- The self-existence of God

- The omnipotence of God

- The unity of God

- The reality of divine providence

- The universality of divine providence

- The efficiency of divine providence

- The spirituality of divine worship

- The non-externality of divine worship

- The unity of the human race

- The possibility of a true natural religion

- The dignity of humanity

- The dependence of humanity

- The absurdity of idols and idol worship

- The essential graciousness of God's dealings with humanity

- The duty of immediate repentance

- The certainty of a day of judgment

- The exaltation of Jesus Christ to the office of supreme judge

- The reality of a future life

Here Paul corrected the errors of:

- Atheism, or the dogma that there is no God

- Pantheism, or the belief that everything is God

- Materialism, or the notion that the world is eternal

- Fatalism, or the superstition that no intelligence presides over the universe, but all things come to pass by necessity or chance

- Polytheism, or the fancy that there are many gods

- Ritualism, or the imagination that God can be honored by purely external performances

- Evolutionism, or the hypothesis that man is a product of natural forces

- Optimism, or the delusion that, in this best possible world, man has no sin of which to repent

- Unitarianism, or the tenet that Christ was an ordinary man

- Annihilationism, or the belief that death is the final end of being

- Universalism, or the sentiment that all will be saved

Talk about skill! Talk about mastering one's field! Talk about industry both in the preparation and in the delivery!

Paul was always engaged in some worthwhile pursuit. Because of his diligence, God was pleased to open up to him doors of opportunity. As a result of Paul's effective execution of his opportunity, God blessed his ministry and at the same time delivered him from fear and anxiety. As Paul himself told the Philippians, "I know both how to be abased, and I know how to abound" (Philippians 4:12).

Paul was so busy he had no time for fear-producing, worry-loaded thoughts. He refused to worry even though he was imprisoned in Rome. Read 2 Timothy 4:13, where he requests that Timothy bring the "books, but especially the parchments." Again, his mind was on what he could accomplish. Industry! This mighty man of God remained industrious right to the end.

What are you waiting for?

Many people piously assert that they are bound to "wait upon the Lord" and to "trust in the Lord" while they sit on the stool of do-nothing and twiddle their thumbs. Now it is true that we must wait upon the Lord and trust in Him. Nevertheless, the proof that we are waiting upon the Lord and trusting in Him will be revealed in our "always abounding in the work of the Lord" (1 Corinthians 15:58).

By industry I refer to activity with a worthwhile purpose, directed toward a worthwhile goal. This is essential to the poise that conquers worry, since you cannot fasten your mind upon two things at once. You cannot throw all your energies into God-glorifying activity while at the same time focusing your attention upon fear-producing thoughts.

Death is characterized by inaction, life by action. As death approaches, action decreases. It has often been noted, in fact, that decreasing activity hastens death. Do you not know some people who were in good health until their retirement, and then suddenly fell ill and died? The transition from work to inactivity was too much for them. It was in their nature to work. Deprived of the opportunity to be industrious, they had no further reason to live.

There are some who rationalize their idleness by saying they are advanced in years—that they have worked all their lives and now deserve a rest. Don't think to immunize yourself so naively from the responsibility of being industrious. Look how many great personalities remained active and productive well into their so-called dotage:

- Golda Meir was leading the modern nation of Israel at the age of 76.

- Cornelius Vanderbilt spent most of his life in ferry transport. He built most of his railroads when he was well over 70, making his hundreds of millions at an age when most men have retired.

- The German philosopher Immanuel Kant wrote some of his greatest works when he was past 70.

- Johann Goethe wrote the second part of *Faust* after he was 80.

- Victor Hugo astounded the world with some of his finest writings after his eightieth birthday.

- Alfred Lord Tennyson was 83 when he wrote his poem "Crossing the Bar."

- Viscount Palmerston was Prime Minister of England at 81, William Gladstone at 83.

- Bismarck was vigorously administering the affairs of the German empire at 74.

- Francesco Crispi was premier of Italy at 75.

- Verdi wrote operas after he was 80.

- Titian painted his incomparable *Battle of Lepanto* at 98, his *Last Supper* at 99.

- Michelangelo was still sculpting masterpieces at 89.

- Claude Monet was still painting great masterpieces after 85.

More years, more creativity

I believe that one of the reasons Sir Winston Churchill and General Douglas MacArthur lived so long was the fact that they both knew and utilized the value of industry.

People like this don't have time for anxiety. Worry is a time thief, and they refuse to be robbed by it.

Norman Cousins, for years the celebrated editor of *Saturday Review*, more than once asserted his belief in a relationship between creativity and longevity. He illustrated his conviction by referring to meetings he had with two men who, when he visited them, were octogenarians—the musician Pablo Casals and the missionary Albert Schweitzer.

He recalls Pablo Casals at eight o'clock in the morning, just before his ninetieth birthday, being assisted by his young wife, Marta, to the piano. Cousins said that watching Casals move made him aware of the man's many infirmities. He seemed to have rheumatoid arthritis, emphysema, swollen hands, and clenched fingers. He was badly stooped, and his head pitched over as he shuffled forward.

Then Cousins tells how Casals arranged himself at the piano and began to play the opening bars of Bach's *Well-Tempered Clavier*. It appeared as though a miracle were taking place. Casals's fingers slowly relaxed. His back straightened. He breathed more freely. He hummed as he played. Finally, as he plunged into a Brahms concerto, his fingers, "now agile and powerful, raced across the keyboard with dashing speed."

The older octogenarian, Albert Schweitzer, told Norman Cousins, "I have no intention of dying so long as I can do things. And if I do things, there's no need to die. So I will live a long, long time." Schweitzer lived to be 95.

I concluded a long time ago that people who find joy in their work, and who are committed to a life of productive industry, enjoy the kind of poise conducive to good health and longevity. Furthermore, industry is consistent with God's will for your life and mine.

19

POISE THROUGH STEWARDSHIP

It's sad but true that many people will put less in the collection plate at church than they will use to buy a ticket for the movies or buy themselves breakfast. They won't give their money. They won't give their time. They won't give their talents. They are afraid of losing out.

Let me be frank with you. No one has a right to expect blessings from God if, through greed and covetousness, he or she blocks the pathway by which God's blessings come.

God is the owner of all things. We are stewards. God knew that man would contest this fact and so He went to special pains to make His ownership clear in the opening chapters of the Bible. God's name is mentioned 14 times in the first 13 verses, 31 times in the first chapter, and 45 times in the first two chapters of Genesis.

God requires stewardship not because of His need, but because of *our* need. God has no needs: "Every beast of the forest is mine, and the cattle upon a thousand hills. . . . If I were hungry, I would not tell thee: for the world is mine, and the fullness thereof" (Psalm 50:10,12). And again: "The silver is mine, and the gold is mine, saith the LORD of hosts" (Haggai 2:8).

God has a threefold basis for demanding our steward-ship. Read Isaiah 43:1: "Now thus saith the LORD that cre-ated thee, O Jacob, and he that formed thee, O Israel, Fear not: for I have redeemed thee, I have called thee by thy name; thou art mine."

God created us. He redeemed us. And He sustains us.

It is impossible for a man to experience the poise that conquers worry unless he possesses an awareness of God's approval. Without the awareness of divine approval, man is plagued by feelings of guilt and fear. He may belong to an Amazonian tribe unreached by even the faintest echo of the gospel, but because of that moral monitor God has placed in his breast he will know, deep within, that he is responsible to a higher power. Not until he comes to know this higher power personally through the mediation of Jesus Christ will his guilt be resolved and his fears subside.

Many are foolishly trying to get victory over guilt and fear with a battery of psychoanalytic techniques: Freudian expressionism and catharsis, Gestalt therapy, and the like. However it is only God who banishes our fear. For through the instrumentality of the Holy Spirit He gives us a spirit "of power, and of love, and of a sound mind" (2 Timothy 1:7). Not that we always make use of this privilege. It is possible for a Christian to be out of fellowship with God and thus forfeit the poise that is dependent upon our awareness of His approval.

The three principles of God's ownership

God has set out three principles in the Bible about the obligations we owe to Him. These transcend the bound-aries of time, geography, and race.

1. *One day out of seven belongs to God.* This first prin-ciple was made clear in the first chapter of the Bible. It has never changed, though it has often

been disobeyed and denied and abused. We are still required to honor God by recognizing the day of rest.

2. *Substitutionary sacrifice is the only answer to human sin.* This principle also transcends time. Again, we can look back to the early chapters of Genesis. When Abel offered an atoning sacrifice it was in response to this fundamental law and unalterable principle. Hebrews 11:4 tells us that Abel offered his sacrifice "by faith," meaning that there had been a revelation from God concerning it. Now, all sacrifices have had their fulfillment in Christ, "the Lamb of God, which taketh away the sin of the world" (John 1:29).

3. *We are called to stewardship of material possessions.* Please pay attention! If you are inclined to get a little impatient with this emphasis on stewardship and turn over to the next chapter, I implore you to hear me out—or rather, to hear God's Word out. One out of every six verses of the four Gospels has to do with the right and wrong use of material possessions. Sixteen of our Lord's 38 parables have to do with the right and wrong use of material possessions. Don't sin against yourself by ignoring this chapter. Suspend your judgment and "to thine own self be true." Surely more anxiety and insecurity among Christians is caused by deficiency at this point than at any other.

Why is stewardship so important?

In the Garden of Eden, God kept to Himself the tree of knowledge of good and evil. This He did to remind Adam and Eve of their duty of stewardship and of God's right of ownership. They were not to touch the fruit of that tree. In a special sense, it belonged to God. True, everything belongs to God, but a certain proportion of that which He bestows upon us is to be set aside immediately and with no strings attached.

Is it not traditional that the tenant farmer in the Midwest be required to give back to the owner one-fourth of the corn crop? Is it not traditional that the tenant farmer in the South be required to give back to the landowner one-third of the cotton crop? Since God is the owner of all things, is it not fair that we be required to give back to Him a proportion of that which He makes possible?

Remember verse 5 of our text in Philippians 4. The word "moderation" means "fairness," among other things. There is no poise without fairness, and there is no fairness without stewardship of material possessions. This poise that brings peace is significantly dependent upon our obedience to stewardship opportunities.

Some folks think giving is meant to finance the local church, as though it were a tax. But to think this is to miss the whole point. We don't give out of duty. We give from an inner compulsion, returning to God through the tithe, and offerings above the tithe, "as the Lord prospers us." We practice stewardship:

1. *In recognition of God's sovereign ownership.* "Thou shalt remember the LORD thy God: for it is he that giveth thee power to get wealth, that he may establish his covenant which he sware unto thy fathers, as it is this day" (Deuteronomy 8:18). Paul picks up the same point in the New Testament: "What? Know ye not that your body is the temple of the Holy Ghost which is in you, which ye have of God, and ye are not your own? For ye are bought with a price: therefore glorify God in your

body, and in your spirit, which are God's" (1 Corinthians 6:19,20).

2. *In appreciative acknowledgement of redeeming grace.* "For by grace are ye saved through faith; and that not of yourselves: it is the gift of God: not of works, lest any man should boast. For we are his workmanship, created in Christ Jesus unto good works, which God hath before ordained that we should walk in them" (Ephesians 2:8-10).

3. *In surrender of life and talents to the Lord.* "I beseech you therefore, brethren, by the mercies of God, that ye present your bodies a living sacrifice, holy, acceptable unto God, which is your reasonable service. And be not conformed to this world: but be ye transformed by the renewing of your mind, that ye may prove what is that good, and acceptable, and perfect, will of God" (Romans 12:1,2).

When you prepare your tithe, you prepare for worship. In church, as you put the money in the collection plate, you are saying in substance, "This is a tangible expression of my total surrender to Thee. This money that I place in this plate represents my brains, my blood, my abilities—all of the blessings that have come from Thee, for I realize that 'every good gift and every perfect gift is from above, and cometh down from the Father of lights, with whom is no variableness, neither shadow of turning' (James 1:17). It is because of the health, because of the mental ability, because of the friends, because of the various resources that Thou hast given me that I am able to make a living. All that I am and all that I have is Thine. My stewardship of material possessions is but an expression of that fact."

The truth about tithing

The basis of our monetary responsibility is the tithe. Tithing is paying back to God ten percent of the increase. And God doesn't mince His words concerning those who fail to obey. The Bible says that if you fail to pay that ten percent back into the "storehouse" with faithful regularity you are a thief and a robber.

There are those who would try to brainwash people into believing that the responsibility of the tithe was only in force during the days of the law—from the time of Moses to the time of Christ. They will tell you that Malachi 3:10 has no relevance for today because it is in the Old Testament.

The Lord must have known that such mischief would arise. Therefore He introduced the words of Malachi 3:6, "For I am the LORD, I change not. . . ." After these words He calls Israel back to His ordinances, to tithes and offerings, to the storehouse, and to His conditional promise of blessing. The New Testament reaffirms these words of Malachi 3:6 by saying that with God there is "no variableness, neither shadow of turning" (James 1:17).

These same people who say that tithing was for those under the law will, of course, turn in the next moment to Psalm 23 for comfort, to Psalm 32 for guidance, to Job for wisdom, and to Elijah for a pattern of prayer—among many other Old Testament passages.

To be consistent, these people who throw out Malachi 3:10 ought also to throw out John 3:16. After all, this too was spoken prior to the time that redemption was completed by our Lord on the cross of Calvary.

In fact, tithing was not a product of the law. Tithing antedated the law. Abraham tithed. The law of the tithe is not an Israelite law. It is a fundamental and unalterable law of God. It is still in force. That is why tithing is commended by Jesus. "Woe unto you, scribes and Pharisees, hypocrites! For ye pay tithe of mint and anise and cummin, and have omitted the weightier matters of the law, judgment, mercy, and faith: these ought ye to have done, and not to leave the other undone" (Matthew 23:23).

Just as Abraham paid tithes to Melchizedek, so we pay tithes to Christ. In Hebrews 7 this truth is made clear. The Son of God who lives and abides as a priest continually after the order of Melchizedek "receiveth tithes"—that is, receives them now! When paying tithes, Abraham acknowledged Melchizedek's sovereignty as a king-priest. Likewise, today when paying the tithe, we acknowledge Christ as Sovereign and Lord. Refusal to pay the tithe is refusal to own Christ as Sovereign and High Priest. Thus one makes Christ not only inferior to Melchizedek, but also inferior to the Levites, the priestly group of Old Testament times.

The tithe was incorporated in the law because it was a principle worthy of divine enforcement. God never repealed the fundamental law of tithing; grace has not annulled it; time has not altered it.

For that reason, Malachi's command concerning the tithe retains all its original force:

> *Will a man rob God? Yet ye have robbed me. But ye say, Wherein have we robbed thee? In tithes and offerings. Ye are cursed with a curse: for ye have robbed me, even this whole nation. Bring ye all the tithes into the storehouse, that there may be meat in mine house, and prove me now herewith, saith the LORD of hosts, if I will not open you the windows of heaven, and pour you out a blessing, that there shall not be room enough to receive it. And I will rebuke the devourer for your sakes, and he shall not destroy the fruits of your ground; neither shall your vine cast her fruit before the time in the field, saith the LORD of hosts. And all*

> *nations shall call you blessed: for ye shall be a delight-*
> *some land, saith the LORD of hosts.*

> —MALACHI 3:8-12

In this command, Malachi makes the practice of tithing a condition for receiving God's blessing in a special way and to a special degree. The implication is clear. When we refuse to pay the tithe we are robbing God, we make ourselves subject to a curse, and we deny ourselves the blessing of God.

Tithing didn't disappear in the New Testament

Grace does not abrogate the law. Grace fulfills the law and goes much further than the most stringent demands of the law. Grace provides the dynamic necessary for fulfilling the law's mechanics. The law told man what to do, but failed to provide him with the capability to accomplish it. Grace provides the dynamic of the Holy Spirit whereby in the strength of God we fulfill the demands of the law, and much more.

Jesus said in Matthew 5:17-20:

> *Think not that I am come to destroy the law, or the*
> *prophets: I am not come to destroy, but to fulfill. For*
> *verily I say unto you, Till heaven and earth pass, one*
> *jot or one tittle shall in no wise pass from the law, till*
> *all be fulfilled. Whosoever therefore shall break one of*
> *these least commandments, and shall teach men so, he*
> *shall be called the least in the kingdom of heaven: but*
> *whosoever shall do and teach them, the same shall be*
> *called great in the kingdom of heaven. For I say unto*
> *you, That except your righteousness shall exceed the*
> *righteousness of the scribes and Pharisees, ye shall in*
> *no case enter into the kingdom of heaven.*

We have already seen how Jesus commended the tithing of the Pharisees. In verse 20 of Matthew 5, the Lord tells us that our righteousness must *exceed* the righteousness of the scribes and Pharisees. Grace fulfills and amplifies the law, instead of destroying and minimizing it.

Proceed further in Matthew 5. The law says, "Thou shalt not kill." Jesus makes it clear that if a man hates his brother he is just as guilty as if he had murdered him. The law says, "Thou shalt not commit adultery." Jesus points out that under grace whosoever looks on a woman to lust after her has already violated the seventh commandment in his heart.

Carry this principle over in the matter of the stewardship of money. How can an enlightened child of God do less under grace than the Jew did under the law? The Jew gave offerings over and above his tithe, too. For instance, if you study the Old Testament, you will discover that the Temple and its equipment were paid for by offerings over and above the tithes.

There is always a question mark in my mind about the person who goes to extremes to prove that we are under no obligation to tithe. What is his motive? In Leviticus 27:30 God makes it clear that "The tithe . . . is the LORD's." Therefore we, as stewards, have absolutely no right to handle it as though it were ours. It must be placed where God says and when God says—namely, in the storehouse on the Lord's day.

The money belongs to God

Jesus said, "Render therefore unto Caesar the things which are Caesar's; and unto God the things that are God's" (Matthew 22:21). In other words, pay your taxes and pay your tithes. Your taxes belong to the government. The proof of this lies in the fact that they are deducted from your pay before you receive it. Your United States income tax is to be paid to the collector of Internal Revenue at a given location.

Suppose you, an American, owed the government an income tax of $1,000. Suppose that you made out your 1040 Form and attached a note to it in which you said:

> *Dear Uncle Sam,*
>
> *You will notice that I owe you $1,000. I am sending $100 to my local postmaster. He is one of your faithful servants and he is having a hard time financially. I am sending $100 to a U.S.O. down in South Carolina. They are doing a magnificent work boosting the morale of your own servicemen, and they need help desperately. I am sending $100 to a nephew of mine who is a sailor with the Seventh Fleet. He is liable to get blown up any time and I think that he needs encouragement. After all, he is one of your faithful servicemen. Then I am sending $200 to the Veterans Administration. After all, they are loyally dedicated to carrying out your will. But, Uncle Sam, just to let you know my heart is in the right place, I am sending the remaining $500 to the collector of Internal Revenue in my area here.*

It's absurd. Why? Because the law of the country does not extend to you the right to decide how the tax money should be distributed. It doesn't belong to you. Therefore your only responsibility is to hand it over.

Here is a man who owes God a tithe of $1,000. But instead of accepting God's revelation that "the tithe is the Lord's," he says, "The tithe is mine. It's my tithe!" Then, acting on that premise, he high-handedly determines the distribution of that money, which is not his in the first place.

He will send $100 to a radio evangelist, another $100 to a Bible school, and another $100 to a missionary.

That is not what God requires. The tithe is to go into the "storehouse," which in this age is the church. Hear the Word of the Lord:

> *Upon the first day of the week let every one of you lay*
> *by him in store, as God hath prospered him, that there*
> *be no gatherings when I come.*
>
> —1 CORINTHIANS 16:2

> *Bring ye all the tithes into the storehouse, that there*
> *may be meat in mine house, and prove me now here-*
> *with, saith the LORD of hosts, if I will not open you*
> *the windows of heaven, and pour you out a blessing,*
> *that there shall not be room enough to receive it.*
>
> —MALACHI 3:10

The word that is translated "store" in 1 Corinthians 16:2 is the same word that was used in the Greek Septuagint to translate "storehouse" in Malachi 3:10. In other words, it would be a correct translation of 1 Corinthians 16:2 to say, "Upon the first day of the week let every one of you lay by him in storehouse. . . ."

Who is the proper beneficiary of the tithe?

Now I should add here that these scriptural truths are set out here by one who doesn't pastor a local church. Rather, I lead a parachurch organization dependent upon the gifts of God's people made above the tithe. Gifts over and above the tithe can be made to Christian causes. But "the tithe . . . is the Lord's." The specific depository is the local church, and it is to be placed there undesignated.

In 1957, when the Lord led me to resign the pastorate to go into the field of evangelism, a dear friend who fought this truth said, "Haggai, now I reckon you will abandon this foolishness about storehouse tithing."

"My change in ministry doesn't mean a change in Scripture or commitment," I replied.

"Follow that notion, and in a year you will collapse for lack of support," he insisted.

Said I, "If this ministry is of God, He'll supply the need."

It was, and He has.

When a man refuses to storehouse tithe his money, he is repeating in kind, if not in degree, the sin of Adam and Eve. In partaking of the forbidden fruit, they took to themselves an authority that was not theirs. That tree belonged to God, not to them. When we do not tithe, we are taking to ourselves an authority that is not ours. We are appropriating money that belongs to God. How then can we expect peace? How can we expect victory over anxiety and freedom from worry? For God and God alone is the Author of peace.

Here is a man who will not honor God by paying the tithe. Yet when his little child becomes critically ill, and the doctors say there is no hope apart from supernatural intervention, that same father will fall on his face before God and say, "O God, this is my child, bone of my bones, flesh of my flesh, blood of my blood. I hand him to Thee. Do what seems good in Thy sight. If it can please Thee, restore him to health and strength and to us."

Such hypocrisy! He is willing to trust God with his own flesh and blood, yet he will not trust God with his silver and gold. Does he think more of his money than he does of his child? How can God honor a man like that? How can God justly bless a man like this who turns his back upon

God as soon as it suits him—turns his back upon God by refusing to tithe.

Here's another illustration: You will remember the passage in Mark 12:41-44, where Jesus sat and beheld how the people cast money into the treasury. You will remember also that a certain poor widow put in two mites. Jesus called His disciples together and said, "This poor widow hath cast more in, than all they which have cast into the treasury" (verse 43).

How could He know? Perhaps they had put part of their tithe into a religious foundation, or some Bible college, or sent it to some radio evangelist. You say, "They didn't have such things back then!" That's true, but it is a fact of history that there were more depositories for the giving of alms in that day than there are today. The others could have said they had given much of their tithe to charitable causes. Jesus judged their stewardship on the basis of what they put into the treasury of the house of God, which today is our own literal, visible, local church.

Consider the process of bringing the tithe.

First you bring the tithe in physically. This couples tithing with worship. The two are inseparable.

Second, you bring *all* the tithe. You don't deduct your doctor's bills, your transportation to and from work, your insurance policies, your gifts to the Red Cross, United Way Appeal Drive, and so forth. You bring a full ten percent of your total increase.

Third, you bring all the tithe into the *storehouse*. When this is done, your responsibility ceases. Even when Paul was trying to get money together for Jerusalem, he didn't tell the Corinthian Christians to send their tithe there. He told them to put their tithe in their local church. Only then did he urge the church to help out its sister congregation in Jerusalem.

You get back what you give out—and more

Now notice the conditional promise of Malachi 3:10: "And prove me now herewith, saith the LORD of hosts, if I will not open you the windows of heaven, and pour you out a blessing, that there shall not be room enough to receive it."

If I could not believe what God says about tithing, I could not believe what He says about anything. It is strange that people will believe what He says about salvation, what He says about heaven, what He says about hell, what He says about baptism, and what He says about soul-winning, yet they will not believe what He says about tithing and the stewardship of possessions.

I know a wealthy man who has set up a religious foundation. He allegedly puts ten percent of his earnings into that foundation and therefore considers himself a tither. However, he does not put the tithe where God says to put it. In addition to that manifest disobedience, one of his corporations borrows the money that is in the nonprofit religious foundation, and does so on highly preferential terms. Therefore he has access to money on which he has to pay no tax—money that he uses to expand his business. You say, "Well, preacher, God is blessing him." Is He? The trouble is that too many people think only in terms of money when they think of God's opening the windows of heaven and pouring out blessings.

I know another man who recently made $40 million in a single year, but because of an ulcerated stomach he can't eat a decent piece of meat. There are some men who would give all of their money if they could buy peace of mind, the respect of their children, the love of their wife.

Once again, let me remind you that from a selfish standpoint it would be to my advantage to preach that a person has a right to place his tithe where he wants, inasmuch as on that basis additional money could be secured to finance my own nonprofit organization. But I know that God would not bless it.

Some time ago a dear friend of mine suggested that a group of businessmen give $10,000 a year out of their tithes to support the ministry God has given me. I thanked him for his generous proposal but said quite frankly, "You are barking up a tree where was never found a possum. I would no more be party to accepting a part of your tithe—a tithe which is not yours, but God's—than I would be party to taking a portion of your income tax—tax which is not yours, but Uncle Sam's."

You say, "What does this have to do with worry?" Plenty! If you went downtown and stole $100 from a merchant, would you have peace of mind? No. You would probably think that people were talking about you every time they looked at you. You would feel uncomfortable whenever you were in the vicinity of the business you had stolen from and to which you are now indebted.

In the fourth chapter of Philippians, from which the textual basis of our formula for victory over worry is found, Paul mentions the liberality of the Philippians. Is it not interesting that the Philippian church was the only church in which Paul found no doctrinal or ethical error? Read the fourth chapter and notice how he commends them for their liberality in the matter of monetary stewardship.

Many people glibly quote verse 19: "My God shall supply all your need according to his riches in glory by Christ Jesus." But may I suggest that the fulfillment of that promise is conditional upon a spirit akin to that expressed by the Philippians, and recorded in the immediately preceding verses?

One of the reasons that many people worry is financial adversity—an adversity sometimes begotten of their own stewardship disobedience. "Honor the LORD with thy substance, and with the first fruits of all thine increase: So shall thy barns be filled with plenty, and thy presses shall burst out with new wine" (Proverbs 3:9,10). These words were written under the inspiration of the Holy Spirit of God.

Failure to tithe is incontrovertible evidence that you are more interested in yourself than you are in the work of the Lord. One of the chief causes of anxiety and worry is self-centeredness. "Where your treasure is, there will your heart be also" (Matthew 6:21).

When your chief concern is not merely how to tithe, but how to give offerings—generous offerings over and above the tithe given to the glory of God—you will experience a joy and a peace the world cannot define. But when you refuse to tithe, you do so either from ignorance or covetousness, and God's Word states that covetousness is idolatry: "Mortify therefore your members which are upon the earth; fornication, uncleanness, inordinate affection, evil concupiscence, and covetousness, which is idolatry" (Colossians 3:5).

Money so easily becomes a tin god. We resemble our gods; we assimilate what we conceive to be desirable. When money is your god there is no peace. But if Christ is the Lord of your life—the dominant dynamic of your experience, the overmastering passion of your interests—then you inevitably begin to resemble Him who "is our peace" (Ephesians 2:14). As a result of your fellowship with Him, you will experience the peace only He can give. "Peace I leave with you, my peace I give unto you: not as the world giveth, give I unto you. Let not your heart be troubled, neither let it be afraid" (John 14:27).

Open yourself to the blessings that God promises to those who honor Him with their substance.

20

POISE THROUGH SURRENDER

After hearing a missionary who had returned from China, a young lady walked up to her and said, "I'd give the world to have your experience."

"That," said the missionary, "is exactly what it cost me."

I am impressed time after time when I listen to missionaries on furlough from a foreign field. They have willingly forfeited economic affluence, worldly ease, and the fellowship of relatives and friends here at home. They have a serenity, a poise that bespeaks a peace that cannot be defined—"the peace of God, which passeth all understanding" (Philippians 4:7).

The Word of God commends this kind of surrender — and not just for missionaries:

> *Neither yield ye your members as instruments of unrighteousness unto sin: but yield yourselves unto God, as those that are alive from the dead, and your members as instruments of righteousness unto God.*

> —ROMANS 6:13

*But what things were gain to me, those I counted loss
for Christ. Yea doubtless, and I count all things but
loss for the excellency of the knowledge of Christ Jesus
my Lord: for whom I have suffered the loss of all
things, and do count them but dung, that I may win
Christ.*

—PHILIPPIANS 3:7,8

*He that findeth his life shall lose it: and he that loseth
his life for my sake shall find it.*

—MATTHEW 10:39

To be sure, the person who has totally surrendered himself to Christ fulfills all the other contributory factors to poise that have already been mentioned. All these aspects interlink and overlap; they are arranged like the facets of a diamond. I have been turning the jewel of poise around and around so that light may be flashed from every side of it and viewed from every angle.

There's less hassle on the narrow path

Many times while in the pastorate and even on occasions since entering the field of evangelism, I have been approached by people who said, in substance, "I know that if I yield my life to the Lord He is going to make me preach, and I don't want to do it." With some it wasn't preaching, but some other sphere of service. There are people who apparently are plagued with the misconception that if they surrender themselves to the Lord He will require of them that which they do not want.

This is a trick of the devil. When you surrender yourself to the Lord you will want what the Lord wants for you. God's Word says, "Delight thyself also in the LORD; and he shall give thee the desires of thine heart" (Psalm 37:4). And, "If ye abide in me, and my words abide in you, ye shall ask what ye will, and it shall be done unto you" (John 15:7).

God's Word tells us that if we, as human parents, give good gifts to our children, how much more will our heavenly Father give good things unto them who ask Him (see Matthew 7:11). Imagine your son or daughter coming to you and saying, "Mom and Dad, I want to do everything that will make you happy. I know that you have had much more experience than I, and there are many mistakes that I can avoid by following your counsel and advice. I beg of you to guide me and direct me. To the best of my ability I will follow your suggestions."

Can you imagine retreating into a private room with your wife or husband and plotting together, saying, "Now little Jimmy has put himself completely in our hands. He is at our mercy. Therefore, let us do everything we can to make him as awkward and miserable and frustrated as possible"?

That's absurd. If we would not treat our own children that way, how much more true is it that our heavenly Father would not treat us that way? "If ye then, being evil, know how to give good gifts unto your children, how much more shall your Father which is in heaven give good things to them that ask him?" (Matthew 7:11). "Like as a father pitieth his children, so the LORD pitieth them that fear him" (Psalm 103:13).

With surrender comes poise that conquers worry.

Lot pitched his tent toward Sodom. Too bad. Lot was a child of God. Second Peter 2:7,8 makes that clear. But Lot went his way instead of God's way. As a result of his disobedience he lost—lost dearly. The Lord told him to get out of Sodom. His married daughters, his sons-in-law, and his grandchildren would not leave with him. Parents may take their children to Sodom, but rarely will they get their children out again once they have been there any length of time.

Lot lost his wife. She was turned into a pillar of salt. He lost all his possessions, his position in the city, his prestige. He lost the respect of his two married daughters, who, in a cave, got him drunk and then committed incest with him, whereby he became the father of one son by each of them. Oh, the grief and anxiety that would have been spared him had Lot only surrendered himself to the Lord! He was robbed of the "desires of his heart" because he refused to "delight himself in the Lord."

Surrender begins with a single step

A young mother asked to see me during a series of speaking engagements in a distant city. I told her I did not do counseling. Her pastor, a senior man of godly discernment, pled with me to break my rule and see this lady. I agreed. She was greatly distraught, mentally and emotionally. The anguish of her heart was torturing her body and imprinting her face. She had been under psychiatric care for more than four-and-a-half years, during which time she had been subjected to shock treatments. She, a professing Christian, gave every evidence of sincerely wanting to do the will of God.

After some brief but pertinent questioning, I asked her frankly if there were something that had taken place in her life, whether years ago or more recently, that preyed constantly on her mind. She said there was. It was a sin committed during adolescence. I asked her if she had confessed it to the Lord. She assured me that she had. Since a second person had been involved, and a third knew about it, the thought that her dereliction might surface terrified her. She couldn't stand the prospect that her children, now entering their teens, might find out. She seriously considered suicide.

I said, "I imagine, from my observation, that you have confessed it to the Lord over and over and over—probably a thousand times. Is that right?"

She nodded her head affirmatively.

I said, "You see, actually, you are making God a liar. You confessed that sin once. God promised you absolute forgiveness, as we read in the words of 1 John 1:9: 'If we confess our sins, he is faithful and just to forgive us our sins, and to cleanse us from all unrighteousness.'"

I said, "The reason you are going through this torture arises from your unwillingness to surrender yourself completely to the Lord. You do not trust Him. You are not willing to take Him at His Word. He has forgiven you, but you refuse to believe it. You refuse to forgive yourself. You are making the mistake of thinking that repentance is repining, and that self-examination is brooding. Now then, simply take God at His Word. Surrender your life completely to Him. Surrender the limitations of your finite mind to the assurance of His unchangeable Word. He has forgiven you. Now in complete surrender, believe it. I can't promise the truth will never surface, or that your children will never learn of it. But, by your current brooding, almost psychotic brooding, you are now depriving your children of the mother they need.

"And, remember the promise of our Lord, 'My grace is sufficient for thee: for My strength is made perfect in weakness'" (2 Corinthians 12:9).

Her husband later said, "I don't know what has happened to her, but she is a different woman. She has a sparkle and a vibrancy I have never seen in her before. Even the children remark about it."

Businessmen across the world, petrified by fear and paralyzed by anxiety over reverses in their business, could enjoy business success and more if they would only sur-render themselves to God and take Him as their partner.

Homes, internally divorced, where husband and wife live together under protest in an atmosphere of tension, could become the vestibule of heaven if husband and wife would simply surrender to Jesus Christ. It is trite, but it is nevertheless true that "if their home were built upon the Rock, Christ Jesus, it would not be headed for the rocks of chaos." Here then is the secret of poise: surrender to Christ.

Remember: "I can do all things through Christ which strengtheneth me" (Philippians 4:13). He will strengthen us to observe the laws of self-control, relaxation, scheduling, stewardship, skill, industry, thought control, and enthu-siasm—all the contributory factors in the mastery of poise—if we will only surrender our wills to Him.

Part 4

PRAYER

21

WHY PRAY?

You might as well ask, "Why use a mobile phone?" The answer is that we need to communicate, and prayer is the best "mobile" you will ever have because you can use it anywhere (even in the subway) and it connects you to the Creator of the universe. It is direct and personal.

Paul's formula for victory over worry is praise, poise, and prayer. You cannot omit prayer. That is why Paul's answer goes so far beyond positive thinking. To win over worry, you must effectively connect with God. As Paul says, "Be careful for nothing; but in every thing by prayer and supplication with thanksgiving let your requests be made known unto God" (Philippians 4:6).

Peace is possible only to those who have related themselves to God through Christ, who is the Prince of Peace. The Bible declares: "There is no peace, saith my God, to the wicked" (Isaiah 57:21). By "the wicked" is meant not only the guttersnipes, the ne'er-do-wells, the riffraff of society. The wicked are those who, unrepentant of their sins, have either refused or neglected to come to the Son of God by faith. They have not received Him into their hearts.

Prayer takes us to the heart of life

Read very carefully, for what you are about to read is a staggering truth.

> *And you hath he quickened, who were dead in tres-passes and sins; wherein in time past ye walked according to the course of this world, according to the prince of the power of the air, the spirit that now work-eth in the children of disobedience.*
>
> —EPHESIANS 2:1,2

God's Word here states that until you receive Jesus Christ as your Savior and Lord, you are "dead in trespasses and sins." As one who is dead in trespasses and sins you are dead to God and to every quality inherent in His nature.

What are these qualities? Some of them are holiness, righteousness, love, truth, wisdom, justice, and power. As one who is dead to God you are therefore dead and insensitive to holiness, righteousness, love, truth, wisdom, justice, and power.

Now pause just a moment and think about what that means. To be sure, those who are dead in sin and therefore dead to God have set up standards. Unfortunately they are not God's standards. "Every man is a law unto himself." That explains marital discord, domestic strife, civil factiousness, labor-management antagonism, national crime, and international tensions.

A person dead in sin and therefore dead to God is alive to Satan and to the qualities inherent in his nature. Some of these qualities are sin, hostility, error, folly, injustice, weakness, and fear. A child of disobedience is dominated and controlled by him. Read Ephesians 2:1,2 again: Satan is "the spirit that now worketh in the children of disobedience."

Someone takes issue and says, "Well, I'm not a drunkard. I'm not a murderer. I'm not a sex libertine. I'm not an extortionist. I'm not a troublemaker. I'm not a thief. I'm not a blasphemer." Of course not. It is not in Satan's interests that everyone be a drunkard, a murderer, a sex libertine, an extortionist, a troublemaker, a thief, or a blasphemer. He transforms himself as an angel of philosophic light, moral light, social light, political light, and cultural light. Satan is a master of public relations.

Until you come to Jesus Christ as a self-confessed sinner and by faith accept the salvation that He has provided, you are spiritually dead. Death means separation. Physical death means separation of the body from the personality. By personality I refer to all of the unseen facets of our being, including soul, spirit, mind, and heart. Spiritual death is our separation in this life from God. Eternal death is our irremediable and unalterable separation from God forever.

Now, because you are spiritually dead, you are separated from God. Therefore you have no peace. Nor can you have any peace. You can use the power of positive thinking, resort to Gestalt psychology, or adhere to Freudian therapy, but it all will be to no avail. Your only hope is in Christ, the Prince of Peace, through whom you have access to God.

Life is union just as death is separation. Physical life is the union of the body and the personality. Spiritual life is union with God through Christ.

When you receive the Lord Jesus Christ as your Savior, you do not receive simply a new concept or a new creed, or a new formula for living. You receive a Person. It is "Christ in you" (Colossians 1:27). You receive a new nature. "Whereby are given unto us exceeding great and precious promises: that by these ye might be partakers of the divine nature, having escaped the corruption that is in the world through lust" (2 Peter 1:4).

Eternal life is the life of God in the soul of the believer. For the child of God, that which we call physical death is but a transition from life to life more abundant, from time to eternity, from the finite into the infinite. Therefore when one receives spiritual life he receives in kind, though not in degree, right here and now, everything that he will enjoy in heaven: communion with God, the favor of God, victory over sin, a transcendent love, divine motivation, and peace.

As mentioned, the formula for peace—victory over worry—is praise, poise, and prayer. No unbeliever can have this perfect peace. The prayer of the unrighteous is an abomination before God (see Proverbs 28:9). God will not hear those who persist in unbelief. "If I regard iniquity in my heart, the Lord will not hear me" (Psalm 66:18).

The only way anyone can come to God is through Jesus Christ. "Jesus saith unto him, I am the way, the truth, and the life: no man cometh unto the Father, but by me" (John 14:6). The blind man whom Christ healed in John 9 stated the truth—a truth that is refuted nowhere in God's Word—when he said, "Now we know that God heareth not sinners: but if any man be a worshiper of God, and doeth his will, him he heareth" (John 9:31).

Four facts about prayer

1. *Prayer is a family matter.* It is a matter between God the Father and born-again believers, His children. Worry is a weakness of the flesh. You cannot conquer a weakness of the flesh in the energy of the flesh. It must be done in the power of God. Prayer gives you access to that power.

2. *Prayer is fundamental.* This is because it makes available to you the divine dynamic whereby you master the mechanics leading to victory over

worry. Prayer is essential to praise. Prayer is essential to poise. God shows us what we must do for victory. In response to prayer He channels to us through the indwelling Holy Spirit the ability to do what we ought to do, which is to obey His commandments.

3. *Prayer raises us to God's level.* It takes us into God's atmosphere. It brings us into communion and intimacy with God. Prayer signifies dependence upon God. Without Him we can do nothing. With Him we can do everything. He is the source of our strength. "I can do all things through Christ which strengtheneth me" (Philippians 4:13).

4. *Prayer recognizes God as the source of our resources.* "My God shall supply all your need according to his riches in glory by Christ Jesus" (Philippians 4:19). The Greek says, "Man, know thyself." The Roman says, "Man, rule thyself." The Chinese says, "Man, improve thyself." The Buddhist says, "Man, annihilate thyself." The Brahman says, "Man, submerge thyself in the universal sum of all." The Muslim says, "Man, submit thyself." The twentieth-century internationalist says, "Man, learn the art and practice the principles of peaceful coexistence." But Christ says, "Without me ye can do nothing" (John 15:5). Conversely, with Him we can do anything.

All you need to be is weak

Prayer is the means whereby we make contact with God's strength. Only when we set aside our own strength will the Lord really become our strength. Attempt to float. As long as you exercise your own efforts to keep up, you will go down. Give yourself up to the water and it will immediately sweep under you with its waves and bear you up in its strength. The Lord Himself is our strength. Don't pray, "Lord, give me strength" as though you are asking Him for a quality distinct from Himself. Rather say, "O Lord, be Thou my strength."

Listen to Ephesians 3:20: "Now unto him that is able to do exceeding abundantly above all that we ask or think, according to the power that worketh in us." The word translated "worketh" is from the Greek word *energeo*. And the word translated "power" is the Greek word *dunamis*, from which we get the word *dynamic*. Just as Satan and his "powers of darkness" energize the unbeliever, so God energizes the obedient Christian. He becomes the divine dynamic whereby the believer conquers all things, including worry.

The same power that burnishes each star, points each blade of grass, hurls each wave upon the shore, formed the body of our Savior, raised Jesus from the dead, and will raise our bodies or transfigure them in the hour of glory is the same power that is available to each obedient Christian. This power is made available through prayer.

But remember: This power is available only to those who are weak. God's helpfulness is meted out only to those who confess their helplessness. "And he said unto me, My grace is sufficient for thee: for my strength is made perfect in weakness. Most gladly therefore will I rather glory in my infirmities, that the power of Christ may rest upon me. Therefore I take pleasure in infirmities, in reproaches, in necessities, in persecutions, in distresses for Christ's sake: for when I am weak, then am I strong" (2 Corinthians 12:9,10).

Our strength lies in childlike helplessness. In your helplessness through prayer, cast yourself upon Him who is our strength. The very essence of the meaning of prayer is that you need help beyond your own strength.

The reason many of us do not pray is that we are too strong—strong in our own false, swaggering, blustering strength. We are strong in our own strength, the very heart of which is utter helplessness, emptiness, and weakness.

Worry is an intrusion into God's province. You are making yourself the father of the household instead of the child. You are setting yourself up as the master of God's kingdom instead of the servant for whom the Master provides.

The basis of prayer is man's need and God's ability to meet that need. When you really pray you are confessing your utter helplessness. You are casting yourself completely and wholly upon God. You are delighting yourself in the Lord. Consequently the Lord grants you the desires of your heart.

Our needs are manifold. Our perplexities are multifarious and variegated. Don't worry. Instead, turn your care into a prayer. Follow the example of Paul, who said, "I conferred not with flesh and blood" (Galatians 1:16). Conferring with flesh and blood about your worries instead of taking them to God is a fruitful cause for increased worry.

The woman who found her weakness—and God's victory

Years ago, while I was still in the pastorate, I concluded a Sunday night service with the benediction. Even before the choir's response had ended, an anxious woman rushed up to me and asked if I would talk with her child, who was under the conviction of sin and wanted to be saved.

It was my joy to see that keen and energetic youngster enter into peace with God through Christ. We had prayer together. As I rose to dismiss them, I realized that the mother was in agony, and she looked at me as if to say, "I am in such trouble. Can you help me?"

I asked her if she would like to speak with me. She grabbed the opportunity as a drowning man would grab a life vest. I asked the youngster to step into the next office for just a moment. Turning to the mother I said, "All right. Would you like to share with me the problem that is causing you this grief?"

She burst into uncontrollable sobs. I assured her that having been pastor of a church of over 3,000 members for several years I was now shockproof. I further reminded her that everything would be held in strictest confidence.

Let me stop here long enough to tell you that this lady was one of the outstanding members of the church. She taught a Sunday school class, was prominent in the Training Union and in the Women's Missionary Society. She almost never missed a service. She tithed her money. She knew her Bible. If Gallup had taken a poll of the membership, I am sure this lady would have ranked among the most respected of all members.

Finally, she blurted out her story. I sat transfixed with astonishment as she told the most sordid story of duplicity and sin I ever had heard from a supposedly respectable woman. At the end she nearly screamed out, "Preacher, have I committed the unpardonable sin?"

It was my joy to assure her from God's Word that if she still desired to repent, God would receive her. I assured her in the words of Jesus, who said, ". . . him that cometh to me I will in no wise cast out" (John 6:37b).

For 11 years she had been trying to win in her own strength the battle of life. Though not yet 40 she had already aged considerably. Her health was poor. She was under psychiatric care. Finally she came to Christ, and became a charming, radiant Christian. Her health returned, and her mind lost its shackles of life-destroying worry.

It wasn't until she confessed her helplessness and cast herself wholly upon God that she received strength to live dynamically. Afterwards, as a child of God, she had a prayer life by which she maintained communion with God and kept unclogged the channel through which His strength could be released to her moment by moment and day by day.

Access the efficiency of prayer

Prayer is essential to poise. Recall the story of Daniel. You remember that he had been hounded by the men who were bent upon his destruction. Nevertheless, he did not alter his habit one iota. There was no ruffling of his spirit. He continued to make his prayer unto God three times a day. He prayed in a spirit of deep humility, recognizing his absolute dependence upon God. Was this a sign of weakness? No! It was a sign of strength. To be sure, Daniel put his face in the dust before God, but he did not lose his courage before the wrath of Darius. He sobbed like a heart-broken child when he knelt before his God, but he faced without a quiver the jaws of the hungry lions. What poise!

Prayer is efficient. This fact ought also to induce a greater interest in prayer. Martin Luther was not talking through his hat when he said, "I have so much business I cannot get along without spending three hours daily in prayer." How is prayer efficient?

1. *Prayer is efficient in that it saves time.* It saves time by conditioning you for the day's activities and personal contacts. It saves time by conditioning those with whom you will associate. It saves time in that it makes available to you wisdom, which in turn leads to quick and proper decisions. "If any of you lack wisdom, let him ask of God, that giveth to all men liberally, and upbraideth not; and it shall be

given him" (James 1:5). This of course leads to peace of mind. How many people there are who fret and mope around wasting precious time simply because they don't know what to do or how to do it. The Lord has promised them the needed wisdom, but they either refuse it or neglect to avail themselves of it. The resultant loss of peace and time is incalculable. How ridiculous it is for the Christian to ask for wisdom and immediately terminate his prayer, taking leave of Him who is the Source of wisdom before He has had time to impart it. What would you think of a man who walked into your home and with apparent earnestness asked you a question, but then turned around and walked out before you had time to answer it? Remember, prayer is not a one-way street. It is a two-way street.

2. *Prayer is efficient because it puts you in touch with infinite intelligence.* Prayer will dispel the fogs of human ignorance. It banishes the darkness of self-destructive errors in judgment. People of prayer, regardless of their academic limitations, are the recipients of a proper perspective and a keen understanding imparted to them by Him who is the Truth.

3. *Prayer is efficient in that it makes grace available to you.* This is the grace necessary to block out negative thoughts, distracting attitudes, and worries that torture the mind and damage the body. Prayer helps us with "casting down imaginations, and every high thing that exalteth itself against the knowledge of God, and bringing into captivity every thought to the obedience of Christ" (2 Corinthians 10:5). When your thoughts are Christ's, they are not worry thoughts.

4. *Prayer is efficient in that it enlists divine strength.*
    Thus it enables you to effect the proper execution
    of your God-given responsibilities. While in the
    flesh upon this earth, our Lord prayed before
    every great endeavor.

5. *Prayer is efficient in that it can change negative cir-
    cumstances.* It can lead to the correction of circum-
    stances that both consume time and saddle a
    person with destructive grief. Do you remember
    the prayer of Moses and Aaron on behalf of their
    sister Miriam who was suffering with leprosy?
    How would that story have ended had it not been
    for their prayer?

6. *Prayer is efficient in that it leads to harmony.* Read
    once again the first chapters of the Acts of the
    Apostles. How differently history would have
    been written had it not been for the prayer of the
    120 people in the upper room. The harmony that
    prevailed among them was one of the by-products
    of their prayer lives. We read concerning them,
    "And all that believed were together, and had all
    things common" (Acts 2:44). Worry cannot survive
    in an atmosphere of such harmony.

7. *Prayer is efficient because it is productive of faith.* And
    faith, of course, is the antidote to worry. Faith is
    acting in confidence upon the word of another.
    The one who is faithful in his prayer life acts in
    confidence upon God's Word. He goes to God
    with all his dilemmas, all of his assets, and all of
    his liabilities. He acts in confidence upon God's
    Word, which tells him that if he delights himself in
    the Lord, the Lord will give him the desires of his
    heart. He prays. God answers his prayer. The very

answer is productive of greater faith—of a more eager and a more earnest disposition to act in confidence upon God's Word.

8. *Prayer is efficient because it leads to inner security.* The person who spends time regularly in prayer comes to know in his inmost soul that God's Word is true when He assures us: "I will never leave thee, nor forsake thee" (Hebrews 13:5). The resulting inner assurance leads to much greater efficiency. For instance, I know a man who always insisted on picking up the tab at the restaurant every time he and his friends were eating out. If he went to a ball game with ten or 15 other folks, he insisted on paying the bill. He constantly gave away expensive gifts—gifts he simply could not afford. Why? His dreadful insecurity is the only answer I can conceive. He compensated for the lack of inner security in his mad effort to secure the fervent friendship of a host of people whose gracious responses to his generosity gave him a temporary sense of well-being.

When a man is properly related to God he has within himself all of the ingredients necessary to provide security, joy, and peace, regardless of external conditions. This relationship is maintained only as a man spends time regularly with God.

Why pray? Pray because prayer is the means whereby you permit and invite God to so energize you that you live victoriously and overcome the world, the flesh, and the devil. Yes, pray because through prayer you enlist the power of the Spirit of God to conquer the weakness of the flesh—even worry. When your thoughts are Christ's, they are not worry thoughts.

22
HOW TO PRAY

When I was 20 years old, I was involved in a four-car accident. Litigation proceedings began almost immediately. I needed help desperately. I needed the resources of the greatest accident lawyer in the country. His name was Weinstein. His fee was understandably large. So large that I, as a ministerial student, could not meet it. However, a dear friend came to see me. He was the owner of a large company in Chicago. He said, "Haggai, Weinstein is our lawyer. We retain him. Here, let me give you one of my cards."

On the back of the card he scribbled a note of introduction to Weinstein. Weinstein saw me. He solved my legal problem. Why? Because of a fee I paid? Not at all. He saw me because of the fee paid by my friend.

The Lord Jesus Christ is my Friend "that sticketh closer than a brother." He paid the fee that I could not pay—the penalty of sin. He paid it with His own blood. In His name and on His merits I have access to God, who alone can solve my problems.

Three Greek words for prayer

The first thing to learn about how to pray, then, is to pray in the name of Jesus, and with His strength. But what are the detailed practicalities about prayer? Paul gives us this instruction:

> *Be careful for nothing; but in every thing by prayer and supplication with thanksgiving let your requests be made known unto God.*
>
> —PHILIPPIANS 4:6

Paul uses three different Greek words for prayer in this verse:

- The *first* word, translated "prayer," refers to a general offering up of wishes and desires to God. This word points to the frame of mind required in the petitioner—a mind of devotion. The word refers to unrestricted concourse between human beings and God. That which brings greatest glory to God and profit to you is the habit of prayer. We might call it the Prayer Mood or the Prayer Disposition. It includes adoration, thanksgiving, confession, and intercession.

- The *second* word, translated "supplication," comes from a Greek word meaning "entreaty," a "seeking," "need," "indigence." It refers to an entreaty impelled by a great sense of need, an extreme want. In fact, the verb form of this word in the original Greek text means "to want." Therefore this word refers distinctly to the petitionary prayers that are expressive of personal need. This prayer is a special petition for the supply of wants, an act of solicitation. It refers strictly to an entreaty to God to supply our needs and our wants.

• The *third* word, translated "requests," refers to requests and, even more strongly, to demands.

On the basis of the teaching of Philippians 4:6, it would be well for us to ponder several factors involved in effectual praying.

Praying to Conquer Worry

If you would conquer worry, pray *intelligently*

"Let your requests be made known unto God."

I heard of a certain man who spent six hours in prayer each day. Lest he should go to sleep when on board a boat, he stood upright and had a rope stretched across so that he might lie against it. If he slept he would fall. His object was to keep on for six hours with what he called prayer. What sort of prayer was it? He kept on repeating, "There is no God, but God. There is no God, but God." He repeated the same thing over and over again. He did not plead with God to give him anything. Just as a witch repeats a chant, so he repeated certain words. That is not praying.

If you get on your knees and simply repeat a certain formula, you are speaking only words. You are not praying. Some people are criticized for using beads and fetishes to "say prayers." But there are many Protestants who just as definitely "say prayers" without meaning. They do not pray. They repeat formulas. They say prayers as did the farmer who each night prayed, "O Lord, bless me, my wife, my son John, his wife, us four, no more. Amen." God does not hear you for your much speaking.

Even though on Mount Carmel the wild-eyed multitude cut themselves and chanted repetitiously, "O Baal, hear us!" they were not praying. Let your requests be made known unto God. Get alone with God and tell Him what you want. Pour out your heart before Him. He does not care for high-flown language. Study the prayers of the Bible and you will be impressed that they have no formal phraseology, and there was no fixed and mechanical use of words. Go to God as you go to your mother, your father, or your friend.

Don't think that God will dissipate your worries just because you get on your knees for a spell every morning and night. Pray intelligently. Tell Him your problem. Tell Him that you have sinned, that you have worried. Tell Him that you want victory over it.

If you would conquer worry, pray *definitely*

Indefinite praying is usually halfhearted praying. Indefinite praying is often insincere praying. It is usually a mere formality. There is no burden, no urgency, no overwhelming constraint in indefinite praying. Indefinite praying shows that you are not sure of the will of God. Therefore you know not what to pray for. It often indicates that you are trusting in the *act* of praying rather than in the God who answers prayer.

Our minds are so constituted that we cannot fasten our desires intensely upon numerous things at the same time. Jesus said, "Therefore I say unto you, What things soever ye desire, when ye pray, believe that ye receive them, and ye shall have them" (Mark 11:24).

Now it is impossible to desire strongly that which is not definite.

Your problem is worry. Pray definitely about this problem. Pray definitely that God will give you victory over your distrust of Him. Pray that God will forgive you for intruding into His own province by trying to carry on

His business. Ask Him for the grace to cast all your cares upon Him.

In addition to all this, pray specifically concerning the problems causing your anxiety. If it is a wayward daughter, pray definitely and specifically for God's will to be done in her life and for God to give you the grace in the meantime to live triumphantly.

If it is financial difficulty, pray definitely that God will show you if you have been unwise in the handling of your money. If you have been unwise, ask Him to forgive you. Pray definitely that He will give you wisdom and grace to do what you can. Pray that He will miraculously do what you can't do. Then rest in the truth of Psalm 37:25: "I have been young, and now am old; yet have I not seen the righteous forsaken, nor his seed begging bread."

If you are suffering from a nervous stomach, pray definitely about it. Don't simply say, "Lord, take away my nervous stomach." Find out what are the causes of your condition. Be specific. Be definite. And then let your request be made known unto God. Or, as we could correctly translate it, "Make known your demands."

Every now and then I hear people say, "God heard my prayer, but He answered it a little differently than I was expecting." That is ridiculous. Imagine if I had five sons and I prayed, "Lord, save my five sons." A few days later my neighbor's five sons all go to church and profess faith in Jesus Christ. Suppose that I then said, "Praise God; He answered my prayer. I prayed for the salvation of my five sons and He answered my prayer. He saved the five sons of my next-door neighbor." That is nonsense.

Pray definitely and expect a definite answer. Pray for bread. God will give you bread, not a stone. Pray for fish. God will give you a fish, not a serpent (see Matthew 7:9-11).

If you would conquer worry, pray *persistently*

Don't be afraid to make demands of God. You can make demands because of your relationship with God through Christ. "My God shall supply all your need according to his riches in glory by Christ Jesus" (Philippians 4:19).

God has promised to supply all your needs. You can demand the fulfillment of that promise—with this warning, however. You are not to say, "Lord, supply all of my needs." Rather, you are to specifically and definitely make known those needs one by one. And then pray persistently. Your cares are persistent. Therefore, make your prayers persistent.

Pray to God and then pray again. If the Lord does not answer you the first time, be grateful that you have good reason for praying again. If He does not answer your requests the second time, thank Him that He loves you so much that He wants to hear your voice again. If He keeps you waiting until you have gone to Him seven times, say to yourself, "Now I know that I worship the God of Elijah, for Elijah's God let him go again seven times before the blessing was given."

Count it an honor to be permitted to wrestle in prayer even as Jacob wrestled with the angel during the long watches of the night. This is the way God develops His servants. Jacob never would have been "Israel" had he not wrestled for the blessing from the angel. He kept on wrestling until he prevailed. Then he became a prince of God. Worry cannot exist with this kind of prayer.

In the Gospels, Jesus taught us to pray. Two great illustrations are recorded in the eleventh and in the eighteenth chapters of Luke.

In Luke 11, the man who wanted to borrow bread at midnight is a striking example of the spirit Jesus desires to inculcate. The borrower was in dire need. He was terribly in earnest and would not take no for an answer. Jesus said that when you pray you should be just as earnest and persistent as this man was. You need the blessing of God much more than he needed his three loaves. You are seeking something that means more than bread, and just as the importunity of the borrower finally wins out, so the soul set upon finding God will command His attention and be heard.

God has no time for lukewarm pleas, for easygoing, halfhearted prayers. If the sense of need is not great, if you forget about the matter before the day is over, God will pay little heed to your prayer. If you have something vital at issue, if you are willing to give time and effort, and if you press your claim home to a finish, God will listen. The man who is willing to quit, or who can quit, is not in the condition of mind and heart to appreciate the favor of God. The soul who counts it the biggest privilege on earth to know God, who seeks for Him and His blessings as men seek for silver and gold, will not only be rewarded, but also will be conditioned to estimate rightly what has been received.

Jesus then says, "I say unto you, Ask, and it shall be given you; seek, and ye shall find; knock, and it shall be opened unto you. For every one that asketh receiveth; and he that seeketh findeth; and to him that knocketh it shall be opened" (Luke 11:9,10). This is not the easy passage some people think it is. It does not mean that all you have to do is ask for something and receive it, or to knock and the door flies open. It refers to a life which is one continual search after God, a constant seeking, a daily asking, a habitual knocking.

This is the only antidote to worry, which itself is perpetual. Let your prayer be perpetual. It means that you must desire that which lies behind the closed door intensely enough to knock with unshaken persistence. Jesus is here saying that to such knocking the door will open. To seeking of that sort will come the answer that makes life full and rich.

The parable found in the eighteenth chapter of Luke is even more striking, as it represents a case where the delayed answer is misunderstood. The petitioner is presented in the figure of a poor widow seeking vindication and protection from an unjust judge. The judge is the perfect embodiment of heartless wickedness. No more complete portrait of depravity was ever drawn than this terse phrase: "which feared not God, neither regarded man" (Luke 18:2).

The feeble, insignificant petitioner was scorned. No heed was given, but Jesus said she continued to press her plea for justice until in absolute selfishness and for no other reason the judge granted the request: "Though I fear not God, nor regard man; yet because this widow troubleth me, I will avenge her, lest by her continual coming she weary me" (Luke 18:4b,5).

The argument is this: If a man like that can be moved to do what means nothing to him, will not God hear the continual cry of His people, whom He loves with a boundless compassion? There are long periods when prayers seem unanswered. There are long days of darkness, sometimes years of wearisome waiting, while countless petitions are sent to a heaven that seems deaf and empty. This is the time about which Jesus speaks. He says, "Cry on, God will hear. He is not heartless, neither has He forgotten."

This parable is for the time when faith has staggered and the heart has grown sick with waiting. Let us remember that the longest delay to us may be as the twinkling of an eye to the plans of God. Alexander Maclaren said years ago, "Heaven's clock does not beat in the same note with our little chronometers." Jesus teaches us to pray on. He says we must not quit. We must not doubt. God knows when to answer. He knows the best time and the most fitting place. We can, in all confidence, leave the question of when and where to Him. Of one thing we may be sure: He will answer. Worthy prayer does not become discouraged. It does not surrender. This is the power that defeats worry.

If you would conquer worry, pray in *faith*

Faith is acting in confidence upon the word of another. Faith in God is acting in confidence upon His Word. You were saved that way. It is also in this way you become mighty with God.

You develop faith as you meditate upon God's Word, the Bible. "So then faith cometh by hearing, and hearing by the word of God" (Romans 10:17). Prayer and the Word of God are inseparably connected. "Feasting" on the Word of God is productive of that faith without which prayer is useless.

Through the Word of God the Lord speaks to our hearts and conditions our hearts for prayer. In prayer we speak to Him in faith. So many times in the Scriptures we have passages indicating that the Lord spoke first, after which the one who heard the Word of the Lord spoke to Him in prayer. Read Jeremiah 1:4-6 as an example:

> *Then the word of the LORD came unto me, saying, Before I formed thee in the belly I knew thee; and before thou camest forth out of the womb I sanctified thee, and I ordained thee a prophet unto the nations. Then said I, Ah, Lord GOD! Behold, I cannot speak: for I am a child.*

You remember also Daniel's great prayer. In the first year of the reign of King Darius we see Daniel reading the Word of God. He had in his hand the prophecy of Jeremiah, in which the Lord had promised that the desolation of Jerusalem would last 70 years. After reading this prophetic promise, Daniel turned to the Lord. The reading of the Word of God led to prayer. The reading of God's Word was productive of the faith that made prayer effectual.

The German theologian Bengel had the reputation of being a great man of prayer, one who knew the secret of effectual prayer. One day a fellow believer watched him at the close of the day. He saw the old saint sitting before a large Bible, reading slowly, often stopping, meditating with the silent tears running down his cheeks. After reading and meditating a long time, Bengel closed the Book and began to speak to God in prayer. His heart had been prepared through the reading of the Word. Neglect of the daily reading of the Word of God and meditation on it soon results in neglected prayer as well.

The secret to earnest and effectual prayer—the prayer of faith—is faithful and diligent study of the Scriptures.

Faith is essential to effectual prayer. All real prayer has as its basis a firm faith in a God who responds to the quest of the human soul. But without faith it is impossible to please Him:

> *"For he that cometh to God must believe that he is, and that he is a rewarder of them that diligently seek him."*
>
> —HEBREWS 11:6

We come to God by our hearts and not by our intellects. The first condition of entering into His fellowship is a faith not only that God is, but also that He will be found by the soul who honestly and persistently seeks for Him. God is not found by those who look for Him in the spirit of cold curiosity. He is not found by those who simply desire to extend the range of their intellectual conquest. This is the reason why many self-styled philosophers and many pseudoscientists have been unable to come to any clear conception of God. It was to men of this type that Zophar said, "Canst thou by searching find out God? Canst thou find out the Almighty unto perfection?" (Job 11:7).

When a man says in the pride of his intellect, "I will now see if there be any God," he may turn his telescope upon the farthest heavens and count the myriad worlds that wander in the blue abyss. He may peer among the atoms and divide and subdivide the electrons, but the greatest thing in the universe will still be hidden from his eyes.

The laws of logic, the theories of philosophy, and the investigations of chemistry and physics all have their place and are of great value, but they are not milestones on the road to fellowship with God. The man who can say with the Hebrew psalmist, "My soul thirsteth for God, for the living God: when shall I come and appear before God?" (Psalm 42:2) is more nearly on the road to His presence. The humble man who with simple and sincere faith reaches out after God will find Him while the philosopher is groping in the shadows of theory and the scientist is bewildered with the results of experiments.

If you would enter into the prayer life that conquers care, spend some time each day with the Word of God. The time spent will be productive of faith that pleases God. This time spent will condition you for communion with God, and as you commune with God you will develop ever more confidence in God, and this glorious cycle will continue unabated as long as you live.

You worry. But if you will utilize this formula of praise, poise, and prayer, God will give you peace. He also makes it clear that by prayer you will be given strength to offer praise and to manifest poise. As you pray you will become effective in prayer. Now believe this: Believe that He will give you precisely what He has promised to give you if you will meet the conditions. He will give you peace. He cannot go back on His promise. He is the God "that cannot lie" (Titus 1:2).

Are you one who prays, but actually only says words? While you are asking God to give you victory over worry, are you at the very same time worrying that you are not praying correctly? Are you worrying that maybe you have not met all of the conditions?

Stop psychoanalyzing yourself! Don't be a spiritual hypochondriac. Get your mind off yourself and onto God. Spend enough time in your prayer thanking Him for what He has done and praising Him for who He is. Then you will be conditioned to pray intelligently, definitely, persistently, and in faith.

As you pray, picture yourself a perfectly adjusted, dynamic, radiant personality living in the strength of God and to the glory of God. This is certainly God's will for you. By faith, then, take God at His Word, lay hold upon Him in prayer, and become a personality to glorify Him and bring peace to your mind. You are what you think you are. Stop, therefore, insulting God. Recognize yourself as a redeemed soul. You are a child of the King. You are in league with the Creator of the universe. Recognize yourself as a potential recipient of qualities, attitudes, and resources that will glorify God and bless those around you as you live triumphantly over every worry and care.

If you would conquer worry, pray *privately*

> When thou prayest, enter into thy closet, and when thou has shut thy door, pray to thy Father which is in secret; and thy Father which seeth in secret shall reward thee openly.
>
> —MATTHEW 6:6

God deals with us face to face and heart to heart. You cannot have audience with a king and be engaged with the crowd at the same time. The matters between you and God are too sacred and personal to be laid bare to the eyes of the crowd. Furthermore, prayer calls for such concentration, such focalization, such rallying of powers, that it demands the quiet of the private space. When we pray we are going to share with God things that are intensely personal—secrets of the heart, sins that need to be confessed, yearnings in your deepest soul that need to be whispered into His ear. Also, we must give God the opportunity to speak to us. God's "still small voice" cannot be heard in the clamor of day-to-day living.

Jesus did not mean that no one could pray except within an empty room. He did mean that the doors of the heart and mind must be shut to the world. When you have shut these doors, then you have the space to pray. For in prayer nobody is present but us and God. Even our dearest friend is outside those doors. He or she may be in the same room physically, or sitting on the same pew, but he or she is still outside. We must not allow any distraction. There should be a mental sign up outside ourselves that says, *Engaged in important business with the Almighty. Keep out!*

I tell you: Worry cannot abide when you are locked up with God in the secret sanctuary of prayer.

If you would conquer worry, pray *thankfully*

The kind of prayer that kills worry is the kind that asks cheerfully and joyfully.

Pray, "Lord, I am in financial straits. I bless Thee for this condition, and I ask Thee to supply all my needs."

Pray, "Lord I am sick. I thank Thee for this affliction, for Thou hast promised that all things work together for good to those that love the Lord. Now hear me, I beseech Thee—if it please Thee."

Or pray, "Lord I am in great trouble. I thank Thee for this trouble for I know that it contains a blessing even though the envelope is black-edged. Now, Lord, give me grace as I pass though this trouble."

This is the kind of prayer that kills worry.

23

WHEN TO PRAY

The story is told of two Irishmen, Pat and Mike, who had narrowly escaped death on a sinking ship. They were floundering around in icy ocean waters on a couple of planks. Pat was addicted to the grossest profanity but was willing to repent of it if the Lord would come to his rescue. Mike thought this theology sound. And so Pat assumed a pious countenance and began to pray.

Just before he arrived at the main thesis of his repentant prayer, Mike spotted a ship coming toward them. As delighted as Columbus when he first spotted the North American shore, Mike hollered, "Hold it, Pat. Don't commit yerself. Here's a ship." And Pat immediately stopped praying.

Isn't that that the way many of us are? The only time we pray is when we are in a jam. And as soon as things improve, we forget God. Our model verse is Psalm 50:15: "Call upon me in the day of trouble: I will deliver thee, and thou shalt glorify me." Spiritually speaking, most of us can much better afford adversity than prosperity. Like the Israelites of old, it seems that when our prosperity expands, our spirituality contracts. Like Pat, we call upon the Lord as long as things are going wrong, but as soon as conditions improve we resort to our own resources. The Lord is an escape hatch—nothing more.

Maintaining a spirit of prayer

The tense used in the Greek text of Philippians 4:6 is present imperative. It carries the idea of ongoing action. In effect, Paul is saying, "Don't perpetually worry. Perpetually pray." Let perpetual prayer take the place of perpetual care.

Our little son Johnny breathed only once every two and a half minutes for the first three hours he was in this world. Because of his deficient breathing, inadequate supplies of oxygen reached his brain, with the result that brain tissues were destroyed and body movement impaired.

Many Christians are suffering from the spiritual equivalent of this condition. Prayer is the Christian's breath. When breathing is obstructed, health is jeopardized. When the Christian permits an obstruction in his or her prayer life, spiritual health declines. An inadequate supply of the oxygen of prayer destroys spiritual fiber and impairs Christian effectiveness. If we want to be spiritually healthy, we must pray ceaselessly. As the Word says, "Pray without ceasing" (1 Thessalonians 5:17).

The Christian's prayer life should be one of incessant prayer, "praying always," as Paul says in Ephesians 6:18. This means praying at all seasons and on all occasions. If you would conquer worry, you must always maintain a spirit of prayer. You must live in a prayerful disposition.

Can we really pray ceaselessly?

One of my theological professors, in discussing the meaning of "pray without ceasing," recalled the experience of some ministers he knew.

They had congregated early and were waiting for the Monday morning ministers' meeting. As they talked in the vestibule, this verse was mentioned. Discussion became spirited. It wasn't long until they readily agreed that the verse puzzled them. How could one possibly pray *without ceasing?*

It so happened that a cleaning woman overheard them, and at this point she joined in.

"I always pray," she told them. "When I go to bed at night, I thank the Lord for the joy of resting on His everlasting arms. When I awaken the next morning, I ask Him to open my eyes that I may behold new and wondrous things out of His Word. When I bathe, I ask Him to cleanse me from secret faults. When I dress, I ask Him to clothe me with humility and love for souls. When I eat, I ask Him to cause me to grow on the bread of His Word. . . ."

She continued like this for several minutes, and taught those professional ministers a lesson they never forgot.

Praying without ceasing means keeping one's mind attuned with Christ and attuned to the will of God. You may not be involved in deliberate and conscious contact with God. But you are aware of His presence and of the fact that your life is being regulated by His will. It is much the same as a mother who is attuned to the needs and wants of her infant, even while she is sleeping—for the slightest whimper will awaken her. Likewise, the slightest prompting of the Spirit should immediately get our attention.

Isaiah says, "Thou wilt keep him in perfect peace, whose mind is stayed on thee: because he trusteth in thee" (Isaiah 26:3). Being attuned to God keeps you in the awareness of His presence. And this produces perfect peace. Prayer is thus an essential ingredient of the peaceful lifestyle.

The pages of the Bible are full of the names of men and women who prayed. All those who had power with God were people of prayer. How else would we explain the poise of Deborah, Daniel, or Hannah?

The great example, of course, is our Lord, whose whole life was a prayer. Before He did anything, He prayed. After He did anything, He prayed. He prayed morning, noon, and night. Sometimes He prayed all night. Whenever he was alone He prayed. Prayer was never off His lips and never out of His heart. He was the perfect example of unceasing prayer.

One word of caution. There are those who excuse their lack of a quiet time with God by saying, "I pray all the time. I pray while I am driving the car to work. I pray when I go about my business. I pray all the time, in whatever I do." Now this is all well and good. But it is essential also to spend a set period apart with God each day. You need to be alone with God for at least some of the time, just as you need to be alone with a husband or wife.

Prayer in practice

Charles Simeon devoted four hours each morning to prayer. Charles Wesley spent two hours daily in prayer. It is said that John Fletcher stained the walls with the breath of his prayers. Sometimes he would pray all night. He said, "I would not rise from my seat without lifting my heart to God." Prayer is the powerhouse of your spiritual life. Not surprisingly, Adoniram Judson gave this advice: "Make all practical sacrifices to maintain it."

You may not have hours at a stretch to devote to prayer. That is fine. D.L. Moody never spent more than 15 minutes in prayer. But he prayed often and about everything. As far as is possible, then, ensure that you have time set aside, preferably at the same time each day, to commune with

24

WHAT TO PRAY FOR

One day my father was replacing a burned-out bulb in the taillight of our old car. In replacing the lens he noticed he had lost a little screw in the tall grass. He had an urgent appointment for that night and not much time to spare. He searched and searched for the little screw, but to no avail.

My younger brother Tom, then five or six years old, was playing next door with a friend. Finally Dad called him and his friend over to help find the screw. When Dad told them what he wanted, Tom asked, "Have you prayed about it?"

My father replied, "No, I haven't, Tom."

Tom said, "Well let's pray, Daddy."

Tom then prayed along the following lines: "Heavenly Father, Daddy has lost the screw that he needs for the car. He can't find it and he needs it badly. Help us to find it. Thank you, Jesus. Amen."

Believe it or not, as soon as Tom had finished his prayer, Dad put his hand down in the grass and retrieved the screw. Coincidence? Not at all! It was a distinct answer to prayer.

Nothing is off-limits for prayer

Since you worry about everything, pray about everything. As Paul says in Philippians 4:6, "In every thing by prayer and supplication with thanksgiving let your requests be made known unto God."

You may pray about the smallest thing or the greatest thing. Set no boundaries with respect to God's care. It is a wide-open field. You may pray for the fullness of the Holy Spirit. You may also pray for a new pair of shoes. Pray to God about the food you eat, the water you drink, the clothing you wear.

Does God not attend to the funeral of every sparrow? Has He not numbered the hairs on our heads? Even the things you think of as big are a small matter to him— though He treats them as important. Our entire earth is like a speck of sand on the beach in comparison to the size of the universe. If you worry about the smallest things, pray about the smallest things.

Peter says to pray "casting all your care upon him; for he careth for you" (1 Peter 5:7). The words translated "care" here are two distinct and different words in the Greek. The first is the same term translated elsewhere as "anxiety," which we discussed earlier with reference to worry and the divided mind. The other refers to God's solicitous interest in our highest good. The verse, then, invites us to throw all our mind-dividing worries onto Him, for He is desirous of the best for us. Throw all your worries down. Just like a large suitcase.

There is an old song by Tindley in which the chorus says:

> Leave it there, leave it there.
> Take your burden to the Lord and leave it there.
> If you trust and never doubt,

He will surely lead you out.
Take your burden to the Lord and leave it there.

How to leave your burden

The trouble is, we pretend to take our burdens to the Lord, but instead of leaving them with Him, we take them all home again.

Close friends of our family lived in Darlington, Maryland, in the early 1940s. The husband and father was a classmate of my father during their school days. This Darlington couple had eight children. The mother, whom we affectionately called Aunt Edith, was coming home from a neighbor's house one Saturday afternoon. As she came nearer she saw her five youngest children huddled together in deep concentration of interest and effort. Finally, after several minutes of trying to discover the center of the attraction, she was close enough to see they were playing with baby skunks. Aghast, she cried at the top of her voice, "Children, run!" At which point each child picked up a skunk and ran!

Isn't that exactly what we do with our burdens and cares? We take them to the Lord in prayer, and He says, "Leave them and run!" Instead we hug them so close that the smell of them clings to us and we wonder why our friends find our presence nauseating! Yet no problem we have as a Christian is too great or too small for God to deal with. But, leave the problem with Him. This is a thrilling thought that you will do well to ponder.

A.T. Pierson, a Bible teacher, sat one day with George Mueller, the founder of many English orphanages. Mueller was relating to Pierson some of the marvelous things God had done for the Faith Orphanage in Bristol. As Mueller talked he wrote, and by and by Pierson noticed that he was having difficulty with his pen point. Suddenly Mueller bowed his head for a moment in prayer and then began writing again. Pierson asked what he had been praying about.

"This pen point," replied Mueller. "It's not working properly. This is an important letter, and I was asking the Lord to help me so I could write clearly."

"Dear me," replied Pierson. "A man who trusts God for millions of pounds also prays about a scratchy pen point!"

If George Mueller had been like many of us, he would have become hot and bothered about his malfunctioning pen. Possibly he would have gotten exasperated with the man who sold him the pen or the company that made it. Perhaps he would have indulged in a little morbid reflection as to why he didn't buy a pen of another make instead of this miserable instrument that was causing him so much trouble. Or he might have thrown the pen down in disgust and given up on the letter, with the result that his conscience would have needled him later for not having written it.

In all kinds of ways, stress and anxiety could have been multiplied by this tiny incident. But it wasn't, because George Mueller wasn't afraid to pray over a small matter like a pen.

Anything big enough to worry about is big enough to pray about

This book has talked about a formula for winning over worry. But that formula will not work unless you enlist the power of almighty God. In your prayer ask God for the grace to enable you to rejoice, to control your feelings, to count your blessings.

Ask Him for the grace to respond to ingratitude with serenity. Call upon Him for the grace of becoming genuinely interested in other people. By prayer, call upon God to help you live in the consciousness of His nearness and therefore to display that poise that is the hallmark of God's presence within you.

Through prayer, ask God to give you the grace to "gird up the loins of your mind" so that you might have the mind of Christ. "Let this mind be in you, which was also in Christ Jesus" (Philippians 2:5).

Through prayer you will enlist divine help in the matters of self-control, relaxation, enthusiasm, scheduling, living each day to the full, developing skills, and being industrious. Through prayer, spend time with God until you know His mind and do His will in the all-important matter of stewardship. Through the right kind of prayer life, you will be strengthened to live the surrendered life so essential to the poise that conquers worry.

Through prayer you can duplicate the request of earnest men and women many years ago, who, turning to Jesus, said, "Teach us to pray." The direct answers of God in response to your prayer will give you the strength to battle and conquer the vicious sin of worry. Apart from the blessings of prayer itself there is also a therapeutic value in the actual time spent in quiet before God. Pray about everything. Pray, and win over worry.

Part 5
PEACE

25

PERFECT PEACE

In Philippians 4:6, the apostle Paul tells us to pray, which helps us to conquer worry. Then in Philippians 4:7, Paul adds this:

> And the peace of God, which passeth all under-
> standing, shall keep your hearts and minds through
> Christ Jesus.
>
> —PHILIPPIANS 4:7

The word translated "peace" can also be translated "tranquility," "harmony," "concord," "security," "safety," "prosperity," and "felicity." Worry cannot survive in this kind of atmosphere. Just as worry involves "dividing the mind," so peace involves "uniting the mind"—fastening it upon worthwhile goals and stimulating it with worthwhile motives.

God is the Author of this peace. It is "the peace of God." And God does not confuse us. "For God is not the author of confusion, but of peace, as in all churches of the saints" (1 Corinthians 14:33). And in the Word of God peace and unity go together, for Christians are to endeavor "to keep the unity of the Spirit in the bond of peace" (Ephesians 4:3).

This is a genuine peace begotten of God.

1. *This peace is not possessed by the hedonist.* Such a person takes everything lightly—snaps his fingers, whistles, and sings. This fellow is a heedless, foolish, light-headed, and light-heeled person who for a little while may dance and sing. He simply postpones his sorrow. The day will come when he will give account. The day will come swiftly and with a vengeance.

2. *This peace is not possessed by the stoic.* The stoic braces his nerves. He will be shaken and moved by nothing. Run a knife into him. He feels the pain, but he will not show it. Despite all manner of knocks and blows in the rough-and-tumble world, he has set his face to the wind and will endure without complaining. This may be commendable, but it is not peace.

3. *This peace is not possessed by the epicurean.* The epicurean chortles out, "Let us eat, drink, and be merry, for tomorrow we die." These are not steel-nerved stoics. They live it up, but they know their long-term prospects are poor.

The peace of God is deep-seated and based upon fact. It is not a self-manufactured hallucination designed to color the facts. This peace is based upon the fact of God's all-sufficiency. It is also based upon our willingness to cast ourselves in self-confessed helplessness upon Him—in response to which He lives through us His own life, bringing harmony, purpose, meaning, and poise.

Peace with God, and the peace of God

This distinction is important. "Therefore being justified by faith, we have peace *with* God through our Lord Jesus

Christ" (Romans 5:1). But not every child of God has the peace *of* God. No one can enjoy the peace of God who does not have peace with God. On the other hand, it is possible, as witnessed by the experience of multitudes of Christians, to have peace with God and fail to appropriate the peace *of* God.

This peace *of* God has its foundation in the fact that God doeth all things well. It has its source in the fact that Jesus "will never leave thee, nor forsake thee" (Hebrews 13:5).

Do you remember the story in Mark 4 of our Lord's trip across the Sea of Galilee? He was asleep in the bottom of the boat. The winds became furious. The waves sprang higher and higher in the air. Soon a tempestuous storm was raging. The little boat was perched perilously aloft the crest one moment only to be dashed into the vortex the next. The terrified disciples cried out, "Lord, save us. We perish!" Jesus was asleep! What peace.

When Jesus arose and subdued the storm, He turned to the disciples and said, "Oh, ye of little faith. Why are ye so fearful?" I can hear them muttering, "Little faith? Little faith? We are veteran seamen. We have never seen a storm like this, and you call it little faith!" Ah, yes. You see, Jesus didn't say, "Let us go out in the middle of the sea and get drowned." He said, "Let us pass over unto the other side" (Mark 4:35).

Now, when you have invited Christ into your life and you have turned the helm over to His control and you have heard His words of assurance, "I will never leave thee, nor forsake thee" (Hebrews 13:5), then there is made available to you a peace the world cannot give and the world cannot take away.

The Peace of God

The peace of God is beyond understanding

This may be interpreted in two ways.

First, it may be interpreted as meaning that God's peace is beyond the scope of human comprehension. It is deeper, broader, sweeter, and more heavenly than the joyful Christian himself can explain. He enjoys what he cannot understand.

Second, it may be interpreted as meaning that God's peace exceeds in effectiveness any merely human means of reducing stress. Here is a man who worries. He tries through the efforts of his own understanding to resolve his worries. He fails. He fails miserably. He may resort to stoicism or epicureanism or the power of positive thinking, but he fails. This man comes to God's Word. He responds affirmatively to God's commands. Having entered into peace with God, he now utilizes that formula which gives the peace of God: praise plus poise plus prayer equals peace. Perfect peace is his privileged possession. In this sense, it surpasses understanding in that it far exceeds in effectiveness any strategy devised by human science.

The peace of God is indestructible

It "shall keep your hearts and minds through Christ Jesus" (Philippians 4:7). Paul here brings into union the conceptions of peace and of war, for he employs a distinctly military word to express the office of this divine peace. That word, translated "shall keep," is the same word used in another of his letters and translated "kept . . . with a garrison" (2 Corinthians 11:32).

This peace of God takes upon itself militaristic functions. It garrisons the heart and mind. The peace of God garrisons and guards the whole person in the full scope of that person's thinking, feeling, willing, desiring, and acting. This divine peace can be enjoyed even in the midst of conflict.

This is an indestructible peace that guards and garrisons you against all care, anxiety, change, suffering, and misfortune. It gives unalterable rest in God.

Deep in the bosom of the ocean, beneath the region where winds howl and billows break, there is calm, but the calm is not stagnation. Each drop in the fathomless abyss may be raised to the surface by the power of the sunbeams, expanded there by their heat, and sent on some beneficent mission across the world. Even so, deep in our hearts beneath the storm, beneath the raging winds and the lashing waves, this peace forms a central, life-sustaining, and refreshing calm.

Drops of this calm may be raised to the surface of our behavior by the power of the Son of Righteousness—Jesus Christ, the Light of the World—and expanded there by the heat of the Holy Spirit and sent on beneficent service across the world.

The peace of God is perpetual

The tense used here in the Greek text is future indicative, and the context makes it clear that the peace of God will proceed in continuous and unabated action.

Stop perpetually worrying. Perpetually let your requests be made known unto God. And you will have the assurance that perpetual peace will garrison and guard your mind and heart through Christ Jesus. What an antidote to worry!

The assurance of this peace is conditional upon no outside circumstance, for this peace is possible only through Christ. A life without Christ is a life without peace. Without Him you may have excitement, worldly success, fulfilled dreams, fun, and gratified passions—but you will never have peace!

Horatio G. Spafford was a successful lawyer in Chicago and a member of the Fullerton Avenue Presbyterian Church in that city. In the financial crisis of 1873 he lost most of his property. In the stress and strain of the times, he prevailed on his wife and four daughters to take a trip to France to get as far away from the scene of worry as possible. He booked a passage for them on the *Ville de Havre*. They set sail November 15.

The trip was uneventful, and its hundreds of passengers were enjoying the restful bliss of an ocean voyage. That is, until the night of November 22.

Shortly after midnight the *Loch Earn*, bound for New York, collided with the *Ville de Havre*. In a few minutes, the French ocean liner sank beneath the waves. The *Loch Earn*, which was not damaged by the collision, rescued as many survivors as could be found. Of the 226 passengers on the *Ville de Havre*, only 87 survived.

Mrs. Spafford was among the survivors, but the four daughters perished. As soon as Mrs. Spafford reached land, she telegraphed from France to her husband: "Saved alone. Children lost. What shall I do?"

The Chicago attorney left immediately to join his wife and bring her back to Chicago. It was in the depths of their bereavement that he wrote his one and only hymn, "It Is Well with My Soul." The grief of his terrible loss and the peace he experienced as he and his wife submitted their lives to God's providential dealings are described in the four stanzas of the hymn:

When peace like a river attendeth my way,
When sorrows like sea billows roll;
Whatever my lot, Thou hast taught me to say,
"It is well, it is well with my soul."

Though Satan should buffet, tho' trials should come,
Let this blest assurance control,
That Christ has regarded my helpless estate,
And hath shed His own blood for my soul.

My sin, O, the bliss of this glorious thought,
My sin not in part but the whole,
Is nailed to the cross and I bear it no more,
Praise the Lord, praise the Lord, O my soul!

And, Lord, haste the day when the faith shall be sight,
The clouds be rolled back as a scroll,
The trump shall resound and the Lord shall descend,
"Even so," it is well with my soul.

Christian friend, before you were saved you had no peace, did you? The Christless heart is like a troubled sea that cannot rest. There is no peace for it. Now you are a Christian. The Lord has brought you peace with respect to your relationship with Him and with respect to your outlook on eternity. However, if you are to enjoy the peace of God over daily worries and cares and anxieties, small though they be—"the little foxes spoil the vines"—you must fix your mind upon Him, "looking unto Jesus" (Hebrews 12:2).

Keep your mind "stayed" on Him. This will enable you to fulfill the biblical formula of praise, poise, and prayer. Praise and poise and prayer together will bring you peace, in the grace of God. As Christ lives in you "your peace shall be as a river, and your righteousness as the waves of the sea."

26

WHERE NOW?

During my sophomore year in high school, my English teacher required the class to read the autobiography of Benjamin Franklin.

This book made an indelible impression upon me. Benjamin Franklin concluded that there were 13 areas of his life that he needed to master. He set his goal to do so in a disciplined and scheduled way. He laid out a grid with the 13 "virtues" listed on the left-hand column and the weeks 1–13 across the top. Each week he would major on one "virtue," while also grading himself on how well or how poorly he was doing with the other 12.

With this system, he was able to cover all 13 "virtues" every three months. Toward the end of his life he said he had mastered each of the virtues except order and organization.

Using this book to change your life

A one-time read-through will not correct a lifelong habit pattern. If you're serious about winning over worry—turning a divided mind into a focused mind, learning how to manage stress—you must systematically, and with discipline, incorporate the book's principles into your daily life.

Winning over worry isn't a magic spell. Nor is it a quick fix. It is a skill you master by applying yourself consistently over a period of time.

Think how many times you fell before you mastered the skill of riding a bicycle. Reflect upon the numerous repetitions required in learning a second language. Consider the slow but steady progress that takes a musical novice to the point of becoming an accomplished pianist.

In just the same way you will need to repeat the behavior required for winning over worry until it no longer requires conscious attention, but becomes the expression of your subconscious.

You may find it helpful to use Benjamin Franklin's method of keeping score.

It may be that you have no problem in maintaining the habit of "rejoicing," but spend very little time "counting your blessings." You may feel that you have a much greater ability to help others than you have thus far demonstrated, and you may wish to take concrete steps with time-specific deadlines to master that. Whatever you major on, maximize the power of spaced repetition by putting up this book's PEACE FORMULA cards around your home and workplace.

I prepared my initial lecture on this subject more than 50 years ago. I wrote the book more than 45 years ago. To this day I refer to it as one would refer to a manual. I commend the material in this book not because I wrote it, but simply because it contains what I have learned through Scripture, observation, and personal experience—and because it has worked for me and thousands of others.

Where to get further help

On the last page of this book, you stand at the beginning of a journey. It is a journey that can take you out of needless anxiety and into the fullness of living. If you would like further help or advice, or access to other materials that can help you on your way, I hope you will feel free to contact me.

I personally can be reached at the following postal address: John Edmund Haggai, P.O. Box 921311, Norcross, Georgia 30010-7311, U.S.A.

Even better, visit *www.howonline.com*, where you will find a full range of resources like this book. All of them have been produced by top experts dedicated to helping you learn—and succeed—in life's essential skills. The subjects range from building relationships to mastering money. We aim to provide you with whatever you need to enhance your personal life and career, and do it at the lowest price. At the website, you will be able to download a complimentary PEACE FORMULA screensaver to help you on your way.

Peace be with you—and stay in touch!

General Index

Scripture Index

OTHER BOOKS BY
JOHN EDMUND HAGGAI

How to Win Over Pain
How to Win Over Fear
How to Win Over Loneliness
My Son Johnny
Lead On! (Leadership That Endures in a Changing World)
The Leading Edge
The Steward
Be Careful What You Call Impossible
The Wachersberg Connection
Paul J. Meyer and The Art of Giving
The Seven Secrets of Effective Business Relationships

ABOUT THE AUTHOR

In more than 60 years of public service, John Edmund Haggai has pastored four churches, held crusades around the world, and established an advanced leadership program with over 37,000 alumni in 158 countries. A Christian world statesman, he has criss-crossed six continents, circled the globe nearly 100 times, and met numerous heads of state.

He was born in Louisville, Kentucky, son of a Syrian immigrant and a New Englander whose ancestors settled in America during the 1600s. An alumnus of both Moody Bible Institute and Furman University, John Haggai was named "Alumnus of the Year" by Moody and has received four honorary doctorates.

He has addressed a wide range of audiences, from British parliamentarians to PRC leaders (under the auspices of the CAIFC), the Kiwanis International Convention, the Texas Medical Association, international investment bankers on Wall Street, graduate students at Yale University, and those attending the commemoration of the 25th anniversary of the Korean War in Seoul, Korea. Among his many awards is the 1988 Faith and Freedom Award from the Religious Heritage Foundation of America.

Churches flourished under his leadership, and in 1954–55 his Baptist church registered more conversions and additions by baptism than any church in the 11 leading evangelical denominations of America. More than 420 invitations within an 18-month period affirmed God's call into crusade evangelism. He preached to large crowds in cities around the nation.

During his first trip to Asia in the 1960s, Dr. Haggai realized changes in global geopolitics, brought about by the end of colonialism, required new strategies for world evangelism. The need to mobilize nationals to reach their own people was clear. After much research, prayer, and development, the first advanced leadership seminar was conducted in 1969.

Despite extraordinary family demands (his son suffered from cerebral palsy), Dr. Haggai has established a unique international ministry and written many influential books. This book, *How to Win over Worry*, has sold more than 2,000,000 copies in 19 languages.

John Edmund Haggai and his wife Christine have lived in Atlanta, Georgia, since 1961, but their influence touches millions of people around the world.

PRAISE PLUS POISE PLUS PRAYER EQUALS PERFECT PEACE!

- ✂ -

PRAISE PLUS POISE PLUS PRAYER EQUALS PERFECT PEACE!

- ✂ -

PRAISE PLUS POISE PLUS PRAYER EQUALS PERFECT PEACE!

- ✂ -

PRAISE PLUS POISE PLUS PRAYER EQUALS PERFECT PEACE!

- ✂ -

PRAISE PLUS POISE PLUS PRAYER EQUALS PERFECT PEACE!